about the author

Sheila Stewart is a serial entrepreneur, author, speaker and marketing expert who has learned a tremendous amount by working backwards and in high heels. Over the last 20 years, Sheila has climbed the corporate ladder, created a reputation as a national marketing expert and built an award winning advertising agency.

Sheila's efforts are now focused on helping women entrepreneurs grow their businesses by providing them with the tools, resources and solutions they need. In the spirit of a true pioneer and rebel, she is defying the odds and creating what everyone has said could not be built. She is building the first global organization that will assist women entrepreneurs from the initial funding stage, through growth, while providing support and then through to the exit/sale of the company. Sheila is a competitive rebel at heart that has earned the respect and reputation of being a down to earth entrepreneur that can relate to others.

Sheila currently owns six companies, lives in Denver, Colorado with her husband and continues to grow her high heel collection.

BACKWARDS
in High Heels

SHEILA STEWART

Caboodle Marketing & Publishing

This publication is designed to provide information in regard to the
subject matter covered. In so doing, neither the publisher nor the author
is engaged in rendering legal, accounting or other professional services.
If you require legal advice or other expert assistance, you should seek the
services of a professional specializing in the particular discipline required.

While the author has made every effort to provide accurate information at
the time of publication, neither the publisher nor the author assumes any
responsibility for errors, or for changes that occur after publication.

Caboodle Marketing & Publishing books may be purchased for
educational, business or sales promotional use. For information, please
write:
Special Promotions Department, Caboodle Marketing & Publishing, P.O.
Box 460303, Aurora, CO 80046-0303.

FIRST EDITION
Published by Caboodle Marketing & Publishing, Denver, CO.
Cover design – Afterhours Group, Denver, CO
Photography – Swartz Photography, Denver, CO

Library of Congress: 2009900748
ISBN: 978-0-9788799-1-4
ISBN-10: 0-9788799-1-0
10 9 8 7 6 5 4 3 2 1

$\mathcal{B}$ACKWARDS
in High Heels

dedication

This book is dedicated to every professional woman who has a sparkle in her eye, a passion in her heart, a kick in her heels and a desire to do and be more in life. This book is written to provide the support, guidance and extra chutzpah that so many women desire to help them along a new and fulfilling journey. Cheers to living on the Fun Bus of Life™.

acknowledgements

I want to express gratitude to my husband, Chuck, for always encouraging me to pave a new path for professional women. You have rallied my spirit to believe that I can truly achieve all that I set out to accomplish. Your words of wisdom and guidance over the last nineteen years are invaluable. Thanks for being my best friend, my biggest fan and my true soul mate.

Thank you to my parents, Buzz and Bonnie Gartrell, who are seemingly ordinary people that have had an extraordinary impact on my life. I only hope that I can make you proud of my accomplishments in this world, since all I do is rooted in the principles you instilled in me.

To Rachel Ceccarelli for being a constant reminder of what our greater mission is for professional women. Your support and dedication are sincerely appreciated and your friendship is extremely valuable to me. Thank you for exceeding my expectations. We've come a long way from that July day when you joined the team.

I acknowledge my mentor, Clark W. Trammell, for your words of advice, tips for success and continual leadership skills as we build the first of its kind women's organization. Your voice is one I love to hear as you continuously lead the cheering section for my life's work.

Sincere gratitude to the six girlfriends I have on speed dial…Tonia Lewis, Jennifer LeBrett, Becky Moffitt, Michele Giletto, Renie Cavallari and Sherrie Nattrass. Thanks for always being there to listen when I just need to talk. I am happy to have you in my life and appreciate your continued support.

To Eric and Fedra Meredith, thanks for being such great friends. I appreciate the fact that you truly get me and can creatively bring to life the books, products and marketing materials for all that we do. Cheers to a world full of red Skittles®!

TABLE OF CONTENTS

Introduction   Page IV

Chapter 1   Dump Your Head-Trash™ and Defy the Odds   Page 1
              Estee Lauder

Chapter 2   (COD) Crap Out Date-Prevention is Key   Page 7
              Debbie Fields

Chapter 3   Your Background Doesn't Define You   Page 24
              Dolly Parton

Chapter 4   Get Real—Know the Real You   Page 35
              Queen Elizabeth I

Chapter 5   Are you Deserving?   Page 44
              Oprah Winfrey

Chapter 6   Become a Raging River   Page 51
              Barbara Walters

Chapter 7   Financial Freedom Can be Found in a Bumble Bee   Page 58
              Mary Kay

Chapter 8   Power—Find Yours and Embrace It   Page 67
              Hillary Clinton

Chapter 9   It's a Game   Page 78
              Robin Roberts

Chapter 10   Play Big or Go Home   Page 86
              Estee Lauder

Chapter 11   Ask for Help and Support   Page 95
              Sheila Johnson

Chapter 12   What you Visualize you Materialize   Page 100
             Celine Dion

Chapter 13   Watch the Road Signs   Page 109
             Tina Turner

Chapter 14   Trust Your Intuition   Page 120
             Sara Blakely

Chapter 15   Say No — Create Balance in Your Life   Page 130
             Gladys Knight

Chapter 16   Delegate   Page 139
             Dr. John Gray

Chapter 17   Are You Mentally Fit?   Page 144
             Jackie Joyner-Kersee

Chapter 18   Never Judge a Book by Its Cover   Page 154
             Cathie Black

Chapter 19   Never Give Up   Page 141
             Lucille Ball

Chapter 20   Get on the Fun Bus   Page 170
             Ellen Degeneres

Chapter 21   Well Behaved Women Rarely Make History   Page 174
             Joan of Arc

Every Woman Should Have   Page 182

Notes   Page 184

INTRODUCTION

I remember walking into my office, which was on the 16th floor of the World Trade Center building in Denver, Colorado. It was a cold winter morning and I was clutching my warm cup of coffee trying to filter some warmth into my hands. I took my coat off and turned on my computer. As I sat down at my desk, I looked out at the gorgeous Rocky Mountains with snow glistening on the mountain tops. I was mesmerized, almost like a robot. I sipped my coffee, not taking my eyes off the mountain tops. The gleaming sparkling snow had hypnotized me. It was at that moment that I asked myself the question, "What am I doing?"

I was thirty one years old and had built a successful division for the advertising agency. I was working 12 to 14 hours per day and generating a lot of revenue for the agency. I had put the necessary systems in place within the agency to improve efficiencies with the account executives. I had led teams to create successful campaigns. But, what was I doing?

Have you ever looked back at a moment in your life and just said "Aha, I get it!"? The instance at the time that seems only semi-consequential, but looking back, it turns out to be a pivotal moment in your life. This day in my office was it for me, I realized something while staring at the Rockies.

As I look back on that moment, I realize that I was experiencing a strong sense of disappointment. What attracted me to that particular advertising agency was the woman who founded it. She had a great story of overcoming obstacles and fighting her way to the top. Yet, I remember when I learned more of the ins and outs of how this agency operated. I was disappointed because here was a woman that had a tremendous opportunity to set an example for other women professionals and she blew it.

I look at the path that has been paved for us, as women professionals, and would never dream of taking it for granted. It was that disappointment that spurred me to make a leap and start my own advertising agency.

I appreciate that the female population has come so far over the years from suffrage to equal opportunities in the workplace. We've come even farther since the days of dancing great, Ginger Rogers. The strange thing is, even though we have come to where we are today, women professionals are still faced with many of the concerns and challenges that Rogers faced during her time.

Let's look at some specific examples. There are many memories indelibly marked in our minds of the elegant Fred Astaire and Ginger Rogers. They have been touted as the greatest dancers of all time with their graceful moves across the dance floor that made them seem as one person. With Ginger's dress, she always looked like she was floating across the floor.

Ginger was in the habit of rehearsing in low heels and then when they were ready to film, she would put on her high heels. When they started to film the dance moves in "Smoke Gets in Your Eyes" Fred forgot that Ginger would be in high heels and then they did the backwards three-step turn-jump up the stairs and Ginger nearly lost her balance. This is the scene that Bob Thaves referred to in his cartoon with the Los Angeles newspaper where a woman was standing and there was a promotion on a sandwich board for a Fred Astaire Festival. A woman standing nearby had a bubble caption coming out from her that read, "Sure he was great, but don't forget Ginger Rogers did everything he did backwards and in high heels."

Many people believed that Fred is the one that launched Ginger's career. Fact is, Ginger's first film with Fred was actually her twentieth film and was only Fred's second film. Also, many don't realize that a lot of the fancy dance moves were Ginger's creation. A fun spirited woman that had a flair for being creative with her feet, she often created the moves that made a scene in a movie. Whether it involved wearing roller skates for the first time in a film dance scene or Fred lifting her over a leg as they danced in circles, Ginger was one talented woman.

Yet, much of the real world gives all of the credit to Fred. It was even well noted that one film director only shot Ginger from the back side in order to feature Fred's full face and to put him in the right light.

Ginger was known to have made less than half of what Fred and many other male stars were paid at that time. Yet, she persevered and always remained true to her roots and her values.

As a woman defying the odds nearly every day, she didn't let anything get in her way. With her hectic schedule, it wasn't unusual for her to work 18 or 20 hour days juggling film and Broadway performances. Many of her male counterparts merely handled either film or Broadway and worked less than eight hours per day. Not Ginger, she seized the opportunities and made things happen.

As women, so often we feel like we are living our lives backwards and in high heels. Just as Ginger, we believe we always have to do things better and faster and make great sacrifices along the way. Fact is that we can learn to dance gracefully through life, even backwards and in high heels.

What causes us to get caught in the trap of feeling like we live in a vicious cycle? We often feel like we are running on a wheel, like a gerbil, and the faster we run to get caught up on tasks, the faster the wheel goes and the more crazy and out of control we feel. We get the wheel going so fast that we can't just jump off because we fear that we will get hurt so what do we do, run faster.

Wrong. There are other options. I have worked with thousands of women entrepreneurs across the United States and Canada and have identified the key elements that are critical for every woman's success. I'm going to share those with you in the chapters to come. I also hope that when you finish this book, you will join me in my mission to help women professionals stretch, grow, appreciate their passion and become more than they ever thought possible.

Change your shoes. Change your attitude. Change your life. Cheers to making this a better world all while driving the Fun Bus of Life.

DUMP YOUR HEAD-TRASH™ AND DEFY THE ODDS

"Some people have thousands of reasons why they can not do what they want to, when all they need is one reason why they can."

— *Mary Francis Berry, Professor*

ginger rogers

Ginger Rogers first learned the Charleston dance as a child. One day she went down to the theater to show everyone behind the scenes how well she had mastered the dance moves. They were obviously impressed because her mother got a call on Friday night asking if Ginger could fill in for one of the kids who had become ill. Ginger was torn between fright and love of the theater. She had head-trash even as a child. Many of us do. Head Trash is the little voices that are formed at an early age and are constantly spewing negative thoughts in our head.

Ginger didn't listen to these voices. She chose to overcome her fear and the doubt in her mind and go down to the theater that night. And she was glad she did. That started the wheels in motion and was the launch of her career.[i]

During the debut of Ginger's first musical in December 1929, Ginger fondly remembered how memorable the night was for her. It was thrilling because she started to see what she could do when she stretched the concept of herself and believed in herself. She suddenly felt six feet tall. Her mother always knew she would make it, but Ginger had experienced millions of doubts.

She was at a moment in her life when she clearly understood the magnitude of managing her thoughts. To think that she had come all the way from a Texas Charleston contest to the magic of Broadway was almost unbelievable. She was relishing in the moment because she overcame the doubts and kept at it.[ii]

Ginger was experiencing what I call head-trash. She had to Dump the Head-Trash in order to achieve greatness. What is head trash? Why is it imperative that women dump the head-trash?

Head trash consists of all those little voices that spout off in our head at just the most in-opportune time. They say things like:

- Who do you think you are?
- What makes you think you can succeed in business, your friend failed?
- You're too young.
- You're too old.
- You don't have enough money.
- You don't have the experience.
- You're not an expert.
- And on and on and on and on.

These little voices talk to us on a daily basis and it's completely up to us whether we choose to believe the thoughts or not. Psychologists have reported we have over 32,000 negative thoughts that occur in our minds each and every day and only 8,000 positive thoughts. We clearly have a propensity to be flooded with the negative. Then all we have to do is turn on the television and we are flooded with even more negativity.

What's the real impact of head-trash? It can be significant. Only 2% of the 10 million women owned businesses in the United States generate more than $1 million per year in revenue.[iii] Why is that? I believe that one of the biggest contributors is head-trash.

If we know that we have negative thoughts, then why do we believe them? Why do we let them effect us? Often it is easier to believe than it is to take a risk and challenge. It clearly takes more time, energy and effort to challenge the status quo than to maintain the current path.

Johnny Bench once said, "Slumps are like a soft bed, easy to get into and hard to get out of." That is how we operate. We get into a slump and decide to believe the 32,000 negative thoughts that we have each and every day. Then, before long we have believed the negative thoughts for so long that they become reality to us.

You no longer need to buy in, give in and cave in. It's time as women that we stand tall and make a commitment to dump the head-trash that is holding us back. It won't be easy, but nothing that's worth it ever is.

estee lauder

Estee Lauder set an amazing example for us women entrepreneurs. One thing Estee Lauder was committed to was her blond hair. She always found money for the House of Ash, a swanky salon on the upper West side of New York City. She so enjoyed the salon that she started taking her products with her and dropping in regularly, just to dab creams on women as they were under the hair dryers. After all, what else did these women have to do but try on creams? This was certainly a captive audience for her. One day as she was dabbling cream on a woman, Estee commented on how lovely her blouse was and asked where she purchased it? The woman's response was simple, "It doesn't matter because you will never be able to afford this anyway." Stunned at first, Estee quickly moved to the next woman and kept dabbing creams. By the time she got home, she was furious. She was even more determined to build a company and build wealth. What if Estee had let this nasty comment affect her? She could have easily let the head-trash takeover. "Yes, who do you really think you are? You don't have enough money to market so how do you believe you will ever build a company? You are just peddling your product in a salon. You don't have any money and what makes you think you ever will?"

Yet, she didn't let the head-trash takeover. She became even more determined and used the negative energy as a positive reinforcement. A few years after her salon testing days Revlon chemists analyzed the ingredients in her products and called them "antiquated" and questioned why she would have sunscreen in the products. How did Estee handle this extremely negative and supposedly detrimental news? Here she was and the supposed experts just told her that the formula she was using was antiquated.

She could have easily bought into the negativity and the head-trash. She knew that her Uncle had brought the formula she was using from the old country. She could have easily believed what they said and told herself that it was antiquated and it wasn't unique or new enough. Yet she didn't. She brushed off their so-called expert analysis and became relentless.

She took pride in her product and she knew what it could do for women. She did not buy into the negativity and head-trash that she could have formed around these comments. She used them as fuel for her determination and commitment to continue. What if she had bought into the negativity? What if she had believed the naysayers? Just think if she had given up we wouldn't have the Free Gift with Purchase. And we all know how much we women love the Free Gift with Purchase.[iv]

Estee Lauder is a business icon that started as a small business owner with a dream and a passion. One of the keys for her was to eliminate one of the greatest barriers that could have so easily distracted her and prevented her from creating the global giant that she built.

So often a small business stays small or gets only limited success because of an array of self-imposed limitations and excuses. Our own mind creates the talking characters we all know too well and sometimes we allow the opinions and thoughts of others to creep in. Several very smart people have said that if you think you can do something, you are right. If you think you can't, you are also right. It's the ability to dream and believe in your own abilities that makes things happen and that has to start with eliminating all of the barriers that are getting in your way. What's preventing you from achieving all that you can and being all that you can?

my story

I was vividly reminded of the power of head-trash when I recently found a folder that had my goals and fears listed. It was dated 2000 and as I began to flip through the pages, I saw a list of twenty two fears that I had. As I read through them, I realized that I was obviously dealing with a significant amount of head-trash at that point in my life. I had things such as fear of success, fear of failure, fear of letting myself down, fear that I couldn't make my business work, fear that I would lose everything, and on and on and on.

As I read through the list, it was a refreshing reminder of how far I have come in dealing with my own head-trash. I read each fear and started to chuckle because I would never be afraid of these things today. I know better. That night I wrote in my journal about the gratitude I had for overcoming those fears. I felt bad for myself knowing that I must have been miserable trying to manage all of those fears plus whatever other negative thoughts were manifesting in my mind. At least I had moved far beyond this state of mind.

Success Tip: Once you tame the power of your mind, you have a hold on the rest of your life. Dump your head-trash. Don't listen to those naysayers and always surround yourself with positive people. If you are constantly surrounded with negative friends, then get new friends. We have enough negativity in our lives every day that we don't need other outside forces spewing more negativity.

2

COD (Crap Out Date) –
Prevention is the Key

"In each of us there are places where we have never gone. Only by pressing the limits do you ever find them."

— *Dr. Joyce Brothers*

ginger rogers

Ginger pushed herself hard from an early age. She would end one movie and the wardrobe fittings for the next movie had already overlapped the previous film. Then there were gallery shots, press interviews and party appearances along with the normal twelve and fourteen hour days shooting scenes.

She never seemed to have the time for a dressmaker to measure the hems of her personal dresses or the time to buy the right pair of shoes for a new gown or the time for a manicure. She was trying to juggle all of her personal needs with her professional demands and it finally took a toll on her. In November 1937, she was exhausted and when she finished the re-takes on Having a Wonderful Life, she knew she had to get out of town. She called her mother and made arrangements for a lengthy amount of time in Sun Valley, Idaho. Here she could relax and forget the fact that she was a movie star. No press. No interviews. No set schedule. It was the break she needed. She had to rejuvenate. Even in the 1930's successful women were dealing with crap out dates.[v]

debbie fields

Debbie had hit a wall. She believed like many of us, that energy automatically replenishes itself and that exhaustion was an unacceptable idea that was associated with weakness and lack of ambition. She was able to ignore these feelings for a while as she scurried from one cookie store to another working more than twelve hour days at the age of twenty two. To her, the cookie business had become a monster that was constantly demanding of her and slowly sucking the energy dry.

She believed that real success came to people who are willing to beat their heads against a wall until the wall falls down. She had reached her limit. She had no time for family, no time for her husband and no time for herself. Meals were eaten on the run and the money she was making gave her no pleasure because she didn't have time to enjoy it.

She started to question and doubt and then sheer exhaustion overcame her and she gave up. One of her husband's friends was married to a woman that had become business acquaintances with Debbie over the years so Debbie offered her half of the company. When she broke the news to her husband, he fell off his chair. He knew how hard she had worked to build the company. It was "her baby" and he couldn't bear to see her throw half of the company away. Yet he understood how much stress she was dealing with.

He told her not to go through with the deal and that they would figure out a way to make it work. It certainly got a lot worse for them before it got better. She realized that growing in business or your personal life is not something you do when you feel like it. It happens to you and it makes certain demands on you and those demands must be met. If you wait, you will lose the moment and the opportunity may never rise again.

Her husband thought he could pull her out of the crisis and instead, it sucked him in with her. Banks were scared of their growth and this was in the late 70's and early 80's.

Debbie was exhausted and her husband was just trying to figure out a way to make the banks comfortable so they would increase the credit lines sufficiently for the growth they were dealing with. No luck with the banks so they decided to sell the rights to all Mrs. Fields stores outside California. They knew it would be a compromise, but it felt like a good one. They found a company that appeared to be a good fit and they approached them with the business proposition.

How could they turn this offer down? Mrs. Fields was willing to sell all of these rights for only $150,000. After weeks of unbearable tension and many highs and lows, they received the answer. It was no. The company did not want to purchase the rights. Debbie was crushed. She felt this was her last hope at a life free of the burden the business had put on her.

This became one of the darkest moments for Debbie and it didn't get better in just one day. It took months and she barely remembers that time as she lived through most of it in the midst of sheer exhaustion. She persisted and continued to slug it out day in and day out even when there seemed to be no hope for relief anywhere in sight.

There was no monumental triumphant day that arrived. The dark clouds just started to slowly lift and they started to feel relief. Part of the solution to living through difficult times can lie in other people. Debbie had always viewed herself as an independent woman that could do anything. Yet she realized that sometimes you can't do it all yourself no matter how strong your will to succeed. In the real world people can hurt themselves by adopting a do-or-die attitude that anchors everything on their own will to succeed.[vi]

For Debbie, she was experiencing what we now call a C.O.D. (crap out date). She turned to her husband for support and then started to find other people to surround herself with to help. She had to get past the independent, stubborn person she had become that was determined to conquer the world on her own and started to cherish and value key people around her.

my story

Flashback to the day in my office when I had the epiphany while gazing at the beautiful Rocky Mountains ahead of me. The day I wondered what I was doing working at this job that I really didn't like with principles I really didn't agree with.

Every time we sat in a meeting at this agency, the client would ask how we knew the advertising campaign was a success and the stock, standard answer was to tout the number of awards that the agency had won. I always thought this was wrong, yet never had a better answer. I knew there had to be a better answer, I hadn't figured it out. I didn't agree with this philosophy, yet I had allowed myself to sit in one too many meetings like that.

It was at that moment in my office daze, while mesmerized with the snow, that I made a decision, one that would change my life forever. I decided that I was going to start my own advertising agency. If I could build a division for an existing agency, then why couldn't I build my own firm? I had made my decision so I marched in and resigned.

I felt exhilarated and excited. I was going to be an entrepreneur at the ripe age of thirty one. I was going to be able to set my own hours, take vacation when I wanted, write my own ticket and do things my way. I was certainly caught up in the moment.

I don't remember driving home that night. My mind was so occupied and caught up with what I was going to do, how I was going to structure things and how much fun I was going to have. As I walked into the house, I ran to my husband and blurted out that I resigned. I rattled on and on telling him how excited I was that I was going to start my own advertising agency. I explained how I was going to do things differently, how I could build it, and how much more time I was going to have.

I finally quit talking long enough to look at his face. I could see the glaze over his eyes and the panic in his face. I said, "What's wrong?" He promptly asked how I was going to fund a new business. He then proceeded to ask how we were going to live, what we were going to do for cash flow and how I was going to do this venture on my own.

Leave it to my husband to bring up all of the logical questions. Hadn't he heard me? He had always been supportive of my career decisions, so why was he so negative?

Then reality set in. I had $5,000 in the bank which would in essence last one month. I hadn't planned for this. If I had planned then I would have been saving instead of spending my money on frivolous things. Then panic set in. The head-trash came flooding out. What had I done? How was I going to make this work? How would I find business? What if I failed?

I had a sinking feeling in the pit of my stomach. I was nauseous and I started to cry. I had tears streaming down my face and my husband looked at me and said, "I'm sure you'll figure it out. You always do. You are smarter than the people you were working for so I know you can do it."

That is just what I needed at that moment. Because I was starting to believe those negative voices that were screaming in my head. I still didn't know how I was going to make this work, but I sat up half the night and started mapping things out. I created the mission, vision and values for my company. I started to develop company names and map how I was going to structure things. This late night brainstorming provided the basis and the foundation for my company.

As is typical with most companies, I was let go from my employer immediately and not asked to fulfill my two weeks notice. I had planned on the last pay check being two weeks to add to my bank account and help fund my new venture. I am a marketing person, not an accountant or a human resource expert. That's when I learned that Colorado is an employment at will state and the employer did not have to pay me nor employ me for the two week's notice that I gave. I had counted on that money. What was I going to do?

Driving home, I started to get that same nauseous feeling in my stomach. I remember the little voices in my head that seemed to be talking reason but were really filling my head with the negative thoughts. "What have you done?" "What makes you think that you are experienced enough?" "You are only thirty one years old, you can't do this?"

That was the longest drive home that day. I did a lot of reflecting and talking to myself. People driving by me probably thought I was crazy. By the time I got home, I marched upstairs and sat down at my desk. I pulled out my paper and I got to work. I listed each person I knew and I started in. I called and found out about networking events, I arranged appointments to just visit, I started checking people off the list one at a time.

Three weeks went by and I had met a lot of people, but didn't have any business yet. Real panic set in. I had that sinking nauseous feeling every day. I woke up with it and went to bed with it. I saw our bills adding up and was trying to figure out how we were going to work things out. I contacted a friend of mine and got a data entry project. I remember how thrilled I was because the money would make our car payment. Here I was with a Masters Degree in Marketing and I was working an hourly job because…I had quit at my own will.

But I was excited because I knew I was going to make it. There was something that came over me that assured me. I somehow knew I could survive. Within the next two weeks I had landed a contract that was nearly $100,000. I really knew then that I could survive. I didn't have any staff, but I was happy to work 18 hours a day to do the work because it was for my own company. There was a sense of pride that ran through my body knowing that I had done this on my own. I also knew, deep down that I could do it.

Within another two weeks, I got a phone call from another woman I had met with and she referred me to a company that was looking for an advertising agency. I called Mark, the Executive Vice President, immediately and as I sat at my desk in my home office with my pink fuzzy slippers on trying to stay warm, he informed me that they were interviewing the agency I previously worked for and one other top agency in Denver. I finished the conversation and as I hung up the phone, I started to laugh. If only the other two agencies could see me in my slippers in my home office with no employees talking to the person we were all pitching. It was great comic relief because then reality set in.

I had my first opportunity to pitch a half million dollar account and in order to get in on the review, I had to be ready in less than one week. The head-trash set in and I had little voices telling me that I was too small, I wasn't ready for this, I didn't have employees so who did I think I was going after an account like this, I didn't have the capital to back me in this venture and so on and so on.

As I nervously paced the floor wondering what I had just gotten myself into, I worked myself into an anxiety attack. So I took deep breaths and reassured myself that this was the opportunity that I had been envisioning, it is what I wanted so I had to go for it. I found a small rational side within me that reassured me of my abilities and negated the head-trash that was so quickly overcoming me. I regained my composure and control and set out on a mission to put the right team together. I instinctively knew what the client needed. I knew what I could do, how I could be different and what would set me apart. I just needed the resources.

I put the virtual team together and we met, strategized and created our game plan. We pitched the client and spent well over an hour with them discussing questions, ideas and thoughts. I turned every objection they had into a positive for them. The fact that we had a virtual team allowed me to pull the experts specifically for their project. We didn't have office space so we didn't have the overhead that had to be built into the cost of the work. We were small which made us nimble and able to respond quickly to their needs. We were new which allowed us to focus all of our attention on them as a client. Every objection was turned into a significant positive for them. We were on a roll.

When we left, I was on a high. I didn't know if we would win the account, but I knew that I had achieved a significant milestone. For me, I had doubted my abilities and now I had just proven that I could do this. It was affirmation that I could do what I thought I could do.

My husband and I had planned a short vacation to Las Vegas and with the $100,000 account I won, we decided to keep our plans and take a little break. I was standing in the hotel lobby at the Mirage Hotel when my cell phone rang. It was Mark and he gave me the news. We had won the half million dollar account. It was all I could do to contain myself and be professional. When I hung up the phone, I had goose bumps and tingling feelings throughout my entire body. I screamed at the top of my lungs. People thought I had won the mega bucks jackpot on the slot machine. Little did they know that I had won a jackpot in another sense.

These two accounts set us on our way. I was officially in business and could quit worrying about the money side of things. I could focus on doing what I loved to do and that is the work, the strategy and the marketing. As the years went by, I grew my staff, got office space, hired more contractors and won more accounts.

For several years, we were on a roll. We had won significant accounts and had the opportunity to do advertising campaigns in Southeast Asia, Europe and Canada. We were working with companies such as Ernst & Young, Signator John Hancock and Six Flags. We had been named one of the top five fastest growing woman owned companies in Colorado, one of the top 250 privately owned companies in Colorado and I had been named one of the top 40 professionals under 40 in Denver.

From the outside, one would think that everything was grand, perfect and going according to plan. Yet inside, I was struggling. I had won all of these awards, these accounts, grown the business yet I was working 90- plus hours each week and hadn't had a vacation in five years. What was wrong with this picture? I kept telling my husband that it wasn't going to be this way for much longer. It would level off and things would shift to where I was working less and the team was taking over.

That never happened. I continued to work the horrendous hours each week. My schedule was insane. I would get home at about 6 pm each night and by 7 pm I was done eating dinner and back in front of the computer in my home office starting my day. I would get a second wind about 9 pm and would work until nearly 2 am. Then I would get up at 6:30 am and do it all over again. There were many nights that I didn't even leave the office until after 11 pm.

When the weekend came around, I would work at night and give myself the day to do all of my errands. What a horrible life, but I kept convincing myself that it was what I wanted. It was supposedly my dream. Yet somehow in my dream, I never envisioned it like this. I never envisioned being a slave to my company and struggling this much.

The schedule started to take a toll on me. My personality started to change and I didn't even know it. I would attend board meetings for the various Chamber and charity organizations and I remember women coming up to me asking how things were with the company and me. My standard stock answer was, "Great. Things are going extremely well." I always showed up all put together with my hand bag matching my shoes and my suit neatly pressed, my hair perfectly fixed in the latest style and with a smile on my face.

I looked the part, but I certainly didn't feel the part. Inside I was a mess. I was falling apart and the giant crack in the fake wall that I had been portraying was widening. Who could I talk to? I couldn't talk to the other women business owners because they were people that I wanted to do business with. I was trying to earn their business and if they thought I had a weakness within my business, would they contract with me? I didn't think so and I certainly didn't want to take that chance.

I couldn't talk to my employees because a true leader doesn't talk down. A leader sets an example and walks the vision of the company each and every day. If I put any inclination of fear in them, they may question my abilities as a business owner. I didn't want that.

I couldn't talk to my husband because Chuck, like all other men, wanted to fix the problem. Yet he couldn't fix the problem because I didn't even really know what it was. He couldn't just listen so I didn't bother him with the issues knowing that he couldn't solve the problem.

So, I kept everything bottled up inside. I kept trying to rationalize things in my own head, but it didn't work. It was only short lived and temporary. Every day I grew more and more tired. I was to the point where I would buy two Venti quad shots from Starbucks to get me through the morning. Then I would turn to diet coke in the afternoon to get enough caffeine to keep me going through the rest of the day. Then at night I would brew coffee to spark the second wind I needed.

I was not eating and when I did, it wasn't healthy food. The quickest alternative for me was to just skip a meal rather than eat. When I ate, I would get this sickening feeling so to feel good, I just didn't eat.

I hit a wall over Christmas 2003. My body and my mind were fried. I knew that it was serious just from the way I felt physically. So I took two weeks off and came back the first of the year rejuvenated. I started in again working as hard as I could and doing the same routine.

I guess the definition of insanity (doing the same thing over and over and expecting a different result) didn't really set in. I didn't believe that I would hit another wall. After all I had taken two weeks to rejuvenate myself.

By the middle of the year, I was in trouble. I woke up one morning and could hardly get out of bed. I crawled into the shower. I was so exhausted just from taking a shower that I had to sit down and rest. I got up and put on my make-up and had to sit down again. I got up and fixed my hair and nearly collapsed from exhaustion.

I made my way to the office finally and felt horrible. My joints hurt, my muscles ached and I felt like I had the worst case of the flu ever. I made it through the day and when I got home, I just crawled in bed. I didn't even eat dinner. I could have cared less about food. I was too tired to even think. I believed that I had the flu yet after two weeks I knew it wasn't the flu.

I finally went to the doctor and they ran all types of tests. They came back and told me that everything was normal. My blood work, my thyroid, my blood pressure and everything else that they tested was normal or below normal. I was perfectly healthy. If I was perfectly healthy, then why did I feel so lousy?

No one could answer that question for me. I kept going back and they would guess and tell me that maybe it was fibromyalgia or maybe it was lupus. They didn't know as everything still appeared to be normal. Until one day the doctor looked at me and proceeded to tell me that it was all in my head.

I know why they have laws against violence. I snapped. How could he tell me it was in my head when I physically felt awful. I had persisted for years with my mind over matter attitude so how could it be in my head when I physically could not move?

I was livid. I got in my car and immediately called Chuck. I started yelling on the phone questioning the audacity of the doctor to accuse me of making this up. I was mortified, I was angry and I was devastated.

By the time I got home, Chuck hugged me and then told me exactly what was wrong with me. He looked at me and simply said, "You don't need any doctors to tell you what's wrong with you. You just need to get rid of your company. The stress and pressure is going to kill you. The decision is yours, but I know that's what is wrong with you."

I listened to what he said and then I crawled in bed. I was thoroughly exhausted from the day and the mental fatigue of being told this was all in my head. As I lay in bed, I remember crying and sobbing uncontrollably. How could I have let myself get to this point? I seemingly had everything in the world. I had a great husband, a nice car, a beautiful house, a company filled with employees and I had won numerous accounts. I had accomplished what I set out to achieve so why did I feel so terrible? What was wrong with me? How could I fix the problem when I didn't even know what was wrong with me?

I finally cried myself to sleep and when I got up the next morning, I did the same routine. I repeated my routine for weeks. I would sit in my office in a daze bewildered and wondering what I was going to do. I was miserable yet when people asked, I still maintained that front and smile and mustered up the courage to say, "Everything is going great."

I started to question myself, my abilities, my dreams, my purpose and my reality. Why was I doing what I was doing? Why did I not have a fire in my belly? We would pitch an account and I was almost lifeless and just went through the motions. I had won the big accounts that people told me I couldn't win. I had built a company when people told me I couldn't. I had a long track record of overcoming the obstacles and challenges that faced me.

Why did I not have the drive and the desire? What happened and how could I fix it? At that point in my life, I was lost. I had never felt so alone in all my life. I didn't know who to talk to and I wasn't effectively solving the problem myself so what was I going to do?

I was in the worst position. As women we can solve almost any problem when we know what the problem is. I was in the horrible position of not even knowing what the problem was. How could I begin to fix something when I didn't even know what was wrong?

I started to get headaches and my head felt very full. So I started journaling as a way of getting all the things out of my head and trying to relieve the pressure. The first day I started to journal I remember the flood just pouring out. My hand could hardly keep up with the movement of the pen.

As I wrote, I started to discover things. I started to deal with Chuck's recommendation to get rid of my company. That wasn't an easy decision because it was my baby. I built something from nothing so how could I get rid of it. What would I do next? What did I want to do?

All of these questions arose and it was a scary time. I felt fearful of the unknown and for the first time in my life, I did not know what I wanted to do with my life. I even questioned my purpose on earth. Wondered why I was put on this planet and wondered what I was to do with my life.

The more questions and fears that arose, the more lost I felt. How was I going to get through these issues to find the real root of the problem? I didn't know but I was frustrated enough that I was not going to give up. That was not an option.

As I continued to journal I started to discover parts of myself that I had stifled. Things that I loved yet had covered up. I started to discover how easily each of us are led astray from our core beliefs and passion into a "me too" world. Our society is so easy to get caught up in and yet difficult to get untangled from.

I realized that there were three primary aspects to what I was dealing with.

> The surface
> The emotion
> The passion

On the surface (or at the shoulders) I had put on the face and maintained the image to the world that everything was great. I had the armor plates on and always walked the part that I thought I needed to in order to do my job.

The next level is the emotion. I believe this lies in your chest area. At this level you show the emotions that are purely that. Anger, unhappiness, negativity and frustration were the emotions that I was continuously emitting. I would snap almost instantly at people and express my feelings from an emotional state.

The last level is what you feel in your gut. This is your true passion. It is a fire that is ignited in your belly and when you are operating from a pure state of passion, no one person or thing can stop you from achieving what you set out to achieve. When in full force, it ignites an adrenaline rush that allows you to conquer the world.

For me, I was operating on the surface and in an emotional state. I didn't know what my true passion was. I had lost that fire in my belly and I didn't know how to get it back.

I started to journal to figure out my passion. I started writing down what I loved to do. Situations when I was thrilled, excited and felt exhilarated. I then started to look for commonalities in each of those situations. I looked for the root that was inherent.

What I concluded is that I love to help people. When I am most excited and on a natural high, I have just helped someone accomplish something they thought was not possible. Then I looked at my life. I realized that I had created a monster with my company. I enjoyed helping people as long as their budget would allow. I wanted to help more small business owners, but their budget wouldn't turn on my lights each month.

I had created a situation with my company where I was working solely for the money at the end of the month. I had a monthly nut that was significant and we had to meet that because I had families depending upon me. I was not focused and guided by what I wanted to do but, rather what would pay the bills.

Somewhere along the line I had gotten screwed up and what I built was not what I wanted to build. I was not joyfully working, I was begrudgingly turning people away because they couldn't afford us. That is not who I am and what I am about.

I have always been about helping others. If that was my passion, then why was I in marketing? Was I supposed to be a marketing professional? Was there something else that I should be doing with my life?

When I analyzed this, I realized that marketing was my gift and helping others was my passion. Marketing has always come naturally to me. I can review an advertising campaign or product packaging and almost immediately identify things that can be improved and modified that will drive more revenue.

I realized that I should not ignore my natural talent. I should find a way to combine my natural talent with my passion for helping others. As I reflected back on situations, I realized that helping entrepreneurs is what really excited me.

It was at that moment I realized my husband was right. Yes, I admit that he's right once in a while. In July 2005, I sold off my advertising agency and took a seven month hiatus. I spent the first two weeks just thinking. I would spend all day in my office looking out the window thinking about what was possible, what I wanted to do, daydreaming and letting my mind wonder.

It was the best thing that I could have done. Within three months I had my health back and I was truly rejuvenated. It wasn't a short lived state. I knew that I was on the right track and had done the right thing. I remember having lunch with a dear friend of mine and he looked at me and said, "I'm really glad you are back." The real me was back in action.

I look back and am grateful that I did go through this difficult time. It has allowed me to empower and help so many other women. I know that I have prevented thousands of CODs and that is extremely gratifying for me.

Success Tip: Accept and honor the difficult times in your life. These are the challenges that allow you to improve your future, learn and become a stronger person. If you don't have a COD story, think about the times you had to overcome any tough challenge. Paying homage to these moments each and every day will allow you to have a more successful future.

3

Your Background Doesn't Define You. It is the Foundation that Builds Your Character

"If someone believes in you, and you believe in your dreams, it can happen."
— *Tiffany Loren Rowe*

ginger rogers

Ginger's mother always told her that she was dancing before she was born. Her mother could feel the toes tapping wildly inside for months. Her mother, Lela, moved to Independence, Missouri, in 1911 after leaving her husband. Lela wanted to have Ginger at home so finding just the right house was important to her. She found just the place at 100 Moore Street which was a small four-room house.

As she settled in, she started looking for a job to support herself and her soon-to-be-born child. Nine month pregnant, Lela read a want ad calling for "a lady of quality as secretary for the Sand Company." She promptly went to the company offices and was interviewed by some bearded men and Lela found herself fending off all types of questions. She admitted that she was pregnant and due the end of the month. Lela also went on to say that her husband traveled a lot and she needed to have a job in order for them to make ends meet.

Having answered all of the questions, she promptly put out her hand and said boldly, "I will be able to start August 1st." The men could not refuse her the job. She was persuasive and pleasant. The men agreed and as Lela started walking home, she began to realize how sweltering the heat was that day. Then, she felt a sharp pain and walked into the drug store to call the doctor. She told him to meet her at her home and she would make the two block trek and if she wasn't there when he arrived, she instructed him to look up the street for her.

She had the strength and tenacity to make it home. She was a bit embarrassed and wringing wet when she arrived, but she had made it. On July 16, 1911 in her own home, with no family near her, she gave birth to a seven-and-a-half-pound baby girl named Virginia Katherine McMath.

Lela did just as she promised the bearded men. She promptly began to work on August 1st. She arrived on day one and asked, "Where's the typewriter." The men looked at her astonished because they had not hired a secretary and an infant. Their reaction mimicked the initial interview. They could not resist the 5'1" dynamo that Lela was so confident and persuasive.

She performed her job, raised Ginger in the office and took on extra typing each week for these men, free in hopes of getting promoted. She certainly knew how to take the $6 per week pay and work into a higher wage.

Her mother believed that somehow Ginger knew she was supposed to be a good baby. If she fussed too much or cried uncontrollably, then it would be hard for Lela to keep her job. Ginger was a very good baby and did not create any issues for Lela at her job.

It is true that Ginger Rogers spent her early years on the office floor of the Sand Company in Independence, Missouri. She saw firsthand how hard her mother worked to support them. She understood from an early age that a strong work ethic and hard work is what pays off for people. It did for her mother and Ginger appreciated all that she did for her.[vii]

This provided the foundation for Ginger's strong work ethic and unwavering commitment to long hard hours, almost to the detriment of her health at times. Ginger was never ashamed of where or how she was raised. She was quite proud of the sacrifices her mother made and all that she did to give Ginger a colorful childhood.

dolly parton

Dolly Parton was born dirt poor, literally. When the doctor came to their home to deliver her, her father didn't have money to pay him so he handed him a sack of corn meal. For Dolly, she was one of twelve children that were raised in the hills of Tennessee. Her family didn't have money for most everyday necessities let alone Christmas toys. So her father would whittle wooden cars and trucks for the boys and her mother would make dolls from corn cobs with silk hair and husks for a dress. Each of the children learned to do without and to sacrifice. New was not a recognized word in their vocabulary. Each child wore hand me down clothes. Her mother was always being given scraps of material and that's how she quilted blankets and made coats for the children.

Dolly reflects back on her childhood and realizes that it is what shaped her. She had to be creative in general and was particularly creative with games because they didn't have the traditional board games that other children played with. They had to be imaginative in order to dream that there was more outside the poor area where they lived. Dolly often escaped the reality by reading stories and dreaming. She loved to read and was known to read anything and everything. She would even read the back of medicine bottles, the funeral directory, the Bible and any book she could get her hands on. To this day, she still has a thirst for knowledge.

It was all of the surroundings, exposure, creative imagination and other elements in her life that led her to write and sing. She always had a love for singing, but the experiences where she grew up provided the basis for many of the songs she wrote. She could sing with passion and convey the message clearly because that is what she experienced firsthand. The emotion she conveyed in her songs was from her heart and soul. That is a special ingredient many artists strive for yet she had it inherently in her.

One of her hit songs, "Coat of Many Colors", was written based upon one particular instance as a child. Dolly remembered watching her mother sew and sew on a new coat just for her. Her mother had picked out the brightest colors in the box of scrap material scraps because she felt it complimented Dolly's colorful personality. She sewed and carefully stitched each piece together trying to make the coat not appear to have been made from rags. Her mother spent timeless hours stitching each stitch by hand, trimming each piece carefully, and with each piece of material love was added. She carefully put a lining in the coat and it was finished. Her mother proudly gave her the coat and Dolly was so excited to wear the coat to school. It wasn't a particularly cold day, but her mother let her wear the coat anyway knowing that she wanted to show it off to the other kids.

Dolly proudly walked into the one room school house and started to parade up the aisle looking left and right waiting for the kids to oooh and ahhhh over her new coat. Yet they didn't. Instead boys were sneering and started laughing calling her coat a bunch of rags. She quickly ignored them thinking that they were just boys being boys. She was looking for compliments from the girls. She wanted them to be jealous of her new coat. Yet she didn't get that reaction from them either. Instead, she got laughed at, fingers pointed at her and the kids kept saying that she was just wearing a box of rags.

Dolly was devastated. The teacher asked her to put her coat in the cloak room and Dolly refused. She didn't want to hide what her mother had so painstakingly stitched with love. She wore it the entire school day and was determined to make her mother and God proud. If the kids only knew the Bible story of Joseph that her mother told her as she carefully stitched the coat, they would understand. Then Dolly realized that no matter what she said, the kids would not understand. They didn't live in poverty, and in a world that wasn't filled with things rather in a world filled with love. That was the commodity worth everything to Dolly and her siblings. They didn't know nor appreciate how much work her mother put into making the coat. Dolly raised her shoulders and held her head high as she proudly walked home from school that day. She knew that she had made her mother and God proud and that's all that mattered to her.

This was the basis for the hit song "Coat of Many Colors" that she wrote years later. She could sing it from the heart because she experienced first hand that character building moment when people were laughing at her for being poor and acting proud of a bunch of rags. Dolly even said that when that song became a hit, she went to her mother and offered to take her into the city and buy her a mink coat. Her mother was quick to say that they eat enough varmets that she didn't want to start wearing them too. Besides, her mother didn't know where she would wear a coat like that other than to the pie social. So Dolly gave her the money instead knowing that was her way of thanking her mother for making the coat of many colors that was part of shaping her life and building her character.

Dolly was never ashamed of her background. She was proud of it and claims in many books and interviews that it shaped her life. Today when people ask her what it's like to make a record or movie, she can't answer the question because there is no one answer. Each record and every movie requires creativity. She is thankful that she has the creative talents that have allowed her to flourish in this environment. It is creative talents that were fostered and flourished when she was a child.

Growing up in poverty built the character and creativeness that she has needed to be successful in life. If she hadn't been raised poor, would she have the hit songs for decades? After all it was those experiences that inspired her to write and sing from the heart with pure passion.[viii]

my story

When people learn that I was raised on a farm in a small town, they always seem to be amazed. I will probably never understand that. When I ask them what they expected, most will say New York City or definitely a large city on the east coast.

I learned early on in life that your background doesn't define you, it builds your character. I was raised in a small town in Colorado with only 60 people in the actual town. We had ten kids in my high school graduating class and our school housed kindergarten through twelfth grades in one building.

Many people cannot fathom what that type of life that would be like. Today we are accustomed to the conveniences and hustle and bustle of a city and have no clue as to what a small town is like. I look back on it today and am thankful that is where I grew up.

Growing up I don't know if we were poor or not. We never seemed to want for anything and we moved into a new house my parents built in 1975. It felt like a mansion to me so I don't have a point of reference for how much or little money we had. I know that I have nothing but fond memories of a fun-filled childhood. I also know that my father worked tirelessly to build his business with my mother preparing meals for five children and all of my father's hired help as well as handling all of the bookkeeping for my father's business.

I was twelve when I went to work for the local restaurant washing dishes for fifty cents an hour, cash of course. At that time my father did not have his business. Both parents worked at the local farmer's co-op so I had to drive myself to work each day. I would drive the white Plymouth that I always called a Tuna Boat because of its massive size. I think twenty people could have fit in the car comfortably.

To a twelve year old, it seemed like a boat. I remember that I proudly drove the 1.5 miles of dirt road every day to go to work. I felt like such an adult earning my own money and driving to work. Most of my friends worked for their family on the farm.

Work was a way of life. Don't get me wrong, we worked hard but we also had a lot of fun. So much fun that in today's world we would have probably been in trouble for it all but in a small town, there are a lot of things that are overlooked.

When I graduated high school, I decided to go to college. This was foreign territory for my parents because I was the only one of their five children that had gone. We figured things out together and did a lot of research and reading. I was fortunate to get scholarships to pay for the entire first year of school in Kansas. Then in my second year, I started to work because I didn't have enough scholarship money to pay all of my bills. By the time I was a junior, I decided to transfer to the University of Denver. As a prestigious private school, it was certainly expensive.

My parents didn't have the resources to help me so I found scholarship money, student loans, I did on-campus work study and got a full-time job off campus. I was also a full-time student so I did not have the time nor the money to party. I was seriously focused on school and work.

Even though I worked on campus and full-time off campus, things were tough. That was one point in my life when I felt poor. There were many days when I didn't know how I was going to buy groceries and do my laundry. I was too proud to call my parents for help because I didn't want to seem like I couldn't make it on my own. I remember one particular week when I had three days to go until pay day and I only had one dollar in my wallet with nothing, literally nothing, in my checking account.

I wasn't sure what I would be able to eat, but I went to the grocery store and figured that if my Mom could feed a table of ten, three times a day with little money, I could certainly be creative enough to figure out how to feed myself for three days on a dollar. I wandered the Safeway store aisles pushing the large shopping cart. Why I had a large cart I don't know, I certainly didn't have the money to fill it full that's for sure.

I wandered up and down the aisles, looking at food options and prices. I was trying to think of what would get me through three days. Then I reached the frozen food section and found chicken pot pies on sale three for ninety nine cents. I knew that would be enough for three days because they were filling. I remember proudly putting them into the cart and walking straight to the check out counter. I unloaded those three chicken pot pies and paid the woman with my last dollar. I don't think she probably had seen someone so happy to purchase chicken pot pies. She didn't realize what this meant for me.

This was only topped by the time when I didn't have enough money to pay for laundry. It would cost me nearly twenty dollars for the coin up laundry machines and dryers and I didn't have it. But I also had no clean clothes. So I decided to fill the bath tub and get on my hands and knees and scrub my clothes by hand. If they could do that in the old days, I figured I could do that in modern days. It wasn't the pain in the back of my legs rather it was my pride that hurt the most. I realized how strong (mentally and physically) women were to do this on a regular basis. I smiled and rinsed my clothes and then hung them on the shower curtain rod to dry. Once dried, I ironed them all so that no one would know those wrinkled clothes had been washed by hand in the bath tub.

When you don't have money, you have this sinking feeling in the pit of your stomach. I am not sure if it is fear, hunger pains or anxiety. I remember sitting in the student lounge every day with my friends who purchased sodas, cookies, pizza and other snacks. I had to sit without anything to drink or eat because I didn't even have an extra fifty nine cents to spend on a soda let alone two dollars for a slice of pizza. I felt poor inside, but tried not to convey that on the outside. I always made some excuse and after a while, my friends quit asking me to join them for a snack.

My mother always told me to never give up. There would always be a way around or out of something if you were willing and creative. I certainly have lived with that attitude for years.

I graduated from DU and finished my schooling in exactly four years. It was a lot of work and tirelessly poor days, but I did it. When I entered the work force, I was fortunate to land a job on the fourteenth floor of a high rise building working for the largest hotel management company in the world. I was proud of what I had accomplished, but I also remember being ashamed of the small town I was from. I always simply said I was a Colorado native. I thought that people would judge me and think less of me because of where I grew up.

Just a few years later I realized that was silly. I think it was a matter of confidence in myself. I worked my way through graduate school and developed even more confidence. Once I watched a woman that I worked for at an advertising agency deny that she had grown up in Wichita, Kansas. She was ashamed of her roots and always told people that she was from Denver, LA and New York. I realized then that where you are from is something to be proud of, not ashamed of.

So I started to talk about what a fabulous childhood I had and how much I learned growing up in a small town. Business was done on a hand shake and I learned how to become a leader.

Your background doesn't define you, but rather it builds your character. I have certainly had a lot of character building days over the years since my childhood and know that I survive each one of the situations because of the creativity and thriftiness that I was taught at a young age. We made do, we did without or we figured out a way. That is a life lesson that I am grateful for and can't say that I would have been this blessed if I hadn't grown up in Idalia, Colorado.

Remember, your background doesn't define you, it builds your character and shapes the way that you look at this world. When things are tough, you toughen up and figure out a way. It is these moments that build the character inside of you and what gives you calluses to weather the storm long-term. No matter what your background is, you have talents and assets. Take an inventory and start leveraging them.

Success Tip: Let your roots grow. Telling your story will open doors to others around you who have similar foundations. It creates a bonding moment and increases your network.

(4)

Get Real – Know the Real You

"Always be a first rate version of yourself, instead of a second rate version of someone else."
— *Judy Garland*

ginger rogers

Ginger Rogers knew who she was deep inside. She may have looked meek and mild on the outside, but she could certainly get her feathers ruffled. She would stand her ground when she believed in something and knew that it was the right thing to do. She was a professional and a perfectionist.

The movie was Top Hat and Ginger had the freedom to work directly with the dress designer to create a one-of-a-kind gown for the "Cheek to Cheek" scene. She wanted a pure blue dress and likened the blue to what you would see in an oil painting from Monet. She wanted the dress to be made from satin with myriads of ostrich feathers with a low cut in the back and a high cut in the front.

This was during a time when the movies were made in black and white yet Ginger was a perfectionist and had a vision of what this dress needed to look like in order to accurately compliment the dance scene. The sketch of the dress was perfect. It was satin and form fitting and would take approximately $1,500 worth of ostrich feathers, at the time that was a considerable amount of money for just the feathers for one dress. But Ginger had the latitude to have the dress she wanted created.

On the day of shooting, Fred and Ginger rehearsed in ordinary clothes to mark the various positions for the camera. Then just after lunch they called for her new blue dress to be sent over from wardrobe. Ginger headed for her portable dressing room and as she was walking, she watched the woman from wardrobe carrying this blue flowing feathered creation through the lot as all of the men, including Fred, stared in amazement at this creation.

She even heard them asking, "What is it? A bird, a plane…" And the reply, "No, it's Ginger's dress." She entered her dressing room and the dress had barely been placed on the rack when there was a knock at the door. The director was abrupt in his comments and told Ginger to wear that white gown she had worn in The Gay Divorcee. Ginger's heart sank as she asked, "You mean you don't like this dress?"

The director could only reply by saying that he didn't think it was right for the scene and he insisted that people would not remember the white dress from a previous movie. Ginger disagreed wholeheartedly. She knew her fans and would never approve of her wearing the same dress in two different movies.

She disagreed and as he made the typical director's exit from her dressing room. Ginger knew she was right and that the dress was perfect for the dance scene. Many actresses would have cried, gotten completely emotional or even thrown objects. Ginger could have reacted that way, but she knew herself better than that. She simply called her mother and asked for her to come to the studio lot immediately. She told her that she would explain as soon as she got there.

Her mother arrived and loved the dress. Ginger explained the situation to her mother, Lela and said that no one would even give her a chance to wear it. They just wanted her to replace it. She needed reinforcement from her mother. The director was not going to listen to Ginger on this one. Ginger had developed a reputation for never standing up for herself. She realized that she wasn't going to get anywhere without reinforcement troops, so to speak. Her mother went to the director and explained how she thought the dress was lovely and would be a nice touch in the dance scene.

After they argued and argued, the director kept insisting that they just call up to wardrobe and get another dress. Finally, Lela had enough and she barked, "Then why don't you find yourself another girl." Ginger had opened the door as she heard all of the commotion. Just as she did, her mother reached in, grabbed her hand and they marched past the director and all of the other executives that had gathered in front of her dressing trailer to discuss this feathered creation.

As they were storming down the lot, they heard a voice calling, "Miss Rogers would you come back onto the stage? We'd like to have you rehearse once in the dress…the blue dress." Ginger turned and looked at her mother. Ginger said, "It's either the dress or I go home so wait for me as you may need to take me home yet."

She went to her dressing room and got into her gorgeous gown. As she walked on set, the emotions were high. Fred didn't like her dress and that was obvious as she came on set. As they rehearsed, a few of the feathers did flutter up and annoy Fred and she heard him muttering after the rehearsal as he plucked feathers from his tailcoat. Ginger was determined to wear the dress. It flowed beautifully and was perfect for that song.

The decision was at hand. They reviewed the first take and Ginger could feel that they conceded graciously yet Fred's attitude was still cool and aloof. Ginger knew herself well enough that she needed to stand her ground on this issue. She was a consummate performer and saw what the dress would add to the scene. A few days later, a box arrived with a note that read "Dear Feathers. I love ya! Fred" and it contained a gold feather for Ginger's charm bracelet.

That feathered dress was added to the Smithsonian Institute in 1984. When you know yourself well enough, you can act with conviction and confidence to achieve whatever you want. No matter how trivial it may seem to others, triumph and pride have no size. The executives learned that about Ginger and did not question her abilities and talent in the future as her dress creation made the scene, even though they wouldn't admit it, she knew it.[ix]

queen elizabeth I

When Queen Elizabeth I ascended the throne in 1558, it is historically written that state of the nation was a sorry one. It was summarized as follows:

England lay now most afflicted, embroiled on the one side with the Scottish, on the other side with the French war; over-charged with debt…the treasury exhausted; Calais…lost, to the great dishonor of the English nation; the people distracted with different opinions in religion; the Queen bare of potent friends, and strengthened with no alliance of foreign princess.

When you read this, you can understand that the Queen was facing many of the same challenges that America is facing today. As a woman leader, it was critical for her to know herself. If this were a business, it would have been viewed as one that was failing. Yet to a twenty-five year old Queen, it was a business in need of a turnaround.

Women in Tudor England at that time were regarded as little more than property and often were not treated with nearly as much care. Elizabeth was born a disappointment and spent much of her life dealing with conflict and strife. Yet somewhere deep inside, she obviously had the confidence and will power to continue. She knew who she was.

She was able to overcome the obstacles and build a team around her that would create legendary growth in a country that was certainly in turmoil when she took the throne. Today we talk about a glass ceiling and that women earn less than men. During Elizabeth's time, there was no such thing as recognition of women. The phrase that rang true across the land was, "The Queen is a woman!"

She chose her battles wisely and was not about to attempt to reorder society at that time. She was not a feminist on a mission to change views, she was a woman on a mission to lead a country into change and prosperity. She knew herself well enough that she was comfortable mocking herself. When one diplomat praised her for her fluency in foreign languages, she replied, "It is no marvel to teach a woman to talk, but it is far harder to teach her to hold her tongue."

Self-deprecation was typical and it clearly served a purpose for her. She played the cards well and used the "woman is weaker" perception to her advantage. She was adept at exploiting the strengths and weaknesses of opponents and those around her. She often encouraged men to view her as a weaker person and underestimate her abilities. She much preferred to be underestimated. That served her well over the years.

She combined her own womanly intuition with observation to determine who was worthy of trust and who was not. She found many people that were smart and witty, yet had no sense of good judgment. She was doing by herself what we do today using numerous tools, software and techniques.

She certainly ruled with a positive force and left a legacy that is still being written about. I believe her success was grounded in the fact that she understood herself well and was able to use that keen insight to her advantage in building a team and facing opponents of all types. If she can do that over four hundred years ago then women today should have no problem knowing ourselves, respecting ourselves and building teams that will help us achieve our greatest potential.[x]

my story

The day you realize that you need to know yourself in order to create the most robust team around you is the day that you will take the first step on a new path to greater success. You need to determine your greatest weakness and then you can find the people who have that as their greatest strength. You want to surround yourself with a strong team that will compensate for your weaknesses and when you do this, you will have great success.

It is often difficult to understand and appreciate our individual strengths and weaknesses. However, the more we know, the stronger we are. Years ago I was introduced to the DISC personality profile and after I took the test and read the results, I was hooked. I became an avid believer and an advocate for the product.

As a woman entrepreneur, one of the most difficult things to do is to analyze and be honest about our true gifts and talents. I found that after taking the DISC profile and answering just 23 questions, which took less than ten minutes, the program had identified my personality. The results described exactly how I like to manage people, what frustrates me, the types of tasks and situations that will annoy me and the environment in which I will thrive. The results were astonishingly correct.

As I read through my results, I thought about how I could use this to hire the right people around me to compensate for my weaknesses and to fill in the gaps. I learned more about the test, the personality types and the traits so that I could identify the types of people that I would need on my team.

It worked. Not only did I create a strong organization, I created one where people worked together and complemented each other.

As an entrepreneur, understanding how to create a strong team is often difficult. We are usually left to the normal determining factors, resumes, personalities, etc. However, there is now a quantifiable way to create an organization that works in harmony.

Another advantage of the test is that it removes the emotion from your decisions. There are no right or wrong answers to the questions and there are no right or wrong results. The test merely points out who each of us is, what we like and dislike. All the information can be used to create stronger teams of people striving to achieve a common goal.

Women entrepreneurs can have the confidence when hiring a team of people. Use the test and your gut instinct as the winning combination when you develop the team around you that will lead you to success. If you want the test, email me at TEST@empower180.com and we will send you the instructions. Yes ladies, it is affordable and I will give you a discount on it for purchasing this book.

So how does this test work? For example, I am a high D (dominance) and my secondary quality is I (influencer). As a high D, one of my greatest challenges is that I can be viewed as aggressive and extremely assertive. I am a driven person and can often leave carnage alongside the road as I mow people over to achieve my goals. I certainly do not intend to hurt anyone's feelings, yet my personality is such that it's just my nature if I am not careful. The I is obviously an inherited gene from my father. I love to talk to people, socialize and create networks of people that all work together. My S (steady relater) is actually zero which means I have no patience. So it is unlikely that I would be well suited trying to balance a check book in order to seek out a two-cent discrepancy. My C (compliance) is also very low. I personally believe that rules are made to be broken. I like to color outside the lines. Yet my husband, a former police officer, scores high in this category making for an interesting dynamic.

Therefore, I surround myself with people who have a greater attention to detail and can handle project management for me. I am a firm believer in this testing tool. I know my strengths and weaknesses as an entrepreneur and a wife. Because I am keenly aware of them, I can be proactive and control the types of people that I hire so that I increase the chances of success. I also understand and respect the personality differences that I have with my husband. I know that he is highly compliant so I do not push the issue when he will not even stop the car in a fire zone for one minute. I know that I can be abrasive and assertive so I have to be careful not to run him over and leave him alongside the road as I blaze ahead to achieve my goals.

Knowing yourself is critical because it will help you not only build better teams and relationships, it also will assist you in understanding why a person may annoy you. It's merely because they are your opposite so respect that and then you will understand how to communicate with the person and work with them.

Imagine if Elizabeth I would have had a personality profile test, she could have really accelerated her success and accomplishments. She did it all purely on woman's intuition in reading and identifying people. We have such an advantage today when we combine such analytical tools with our proven women's intuition. We truly can be unstoppable. [xi]

Success Tip: Use a DISC profile or similar tests to assess your abilities then cross reference this with the many "shoes" you wear and responsibility you have. You may find you are fit for a completely different career or, as an entrepreneur, you could be in just the right position now.

5

ARE YOU DESERVING – WHO DEFINES WHAT YOU DESERVE AND DON'T DESERVE?

"I have never felt a moment of guilt about what I have."
— *Oprah Winfrey*

ginger rogers

For years Ginger had been going with the flow. She had numerous contracts that she kept being presented. It seemed as she finished one project, another was waiting in the wings. She often was working on movies by day and on Broadway by night with little sleep in between.

It seemed like each contract was worth more than the last so she never questioned the amount of money that was put on the document. She was always thankful to be working, busy and making money. In 1936, that changed. As she was working with her agent to negotiate the next contract, she decided she wanted her rightful due not only in money but also in roles. She was tired of being Miss Cooperation.

She deserved more and had reached a point where she knew it, believed it and saw it. Her pictures had been making big money and she knew that she had never asked for anything along the way. She had been settling for the roles they gave her. Never questioning those roles or demanding roles more appropriate for her skill set. She had never been absent from a shoot.

This time Ginger took a stance. She demanded the studio pay more and give her more latitude with her roles. Her sense of deserving came from deep inside. Ginger refused to report to the studio until something was done about her contract. There are many that rallied behind her and one in particular that wrote a letter to the president of the studio. In that letter he clearly gave Ginger the accolades she deserved for the hard work, dedication and relentless commitment. He also indicated that $500 more per week certainly wouldn't make a big difference for the studio at the end of the year when the tally had been totaled.

Ginger stood her ground and finally got what she deserved. The studio agreed to draw up a new contract but Ginger refused to show up until she had received it and the contract was signed. From then on, she negotiated the contracts that were presented to her instead of taking what was handed to her first. She had learned that she was making nearly half of what Fred Astaire was making and a fraction of what other actors were making. She had made more films than many others and she also knew deep inside how talented she was.

She reached the point where she realized that no one was going to tell her what she deserved. She knew what she deserved and she was going to stand her ground until she got it.[xii]

oprah winfrey

A 17-year old Oprah Winfrey entered the Nashville Miss Fire Prevention beauty contest and when a judge asked her what she would do with a million dollars, she replied, "I'd be a spending fool." She won the crown and set her career in motion. She didn't win a million dollars but has obviously achieved the status as one of the wealthiest people in the world. The wealth she has amassed is more than many countries' gross domestic product.

She is quoted as saying that she never felt a moment of guilt about what she has. Many women have a hard time understanding that. Many women inherently have difficulty believing they deserve more money, success, fame or anything else in the world. Oprah has said that the thing she is most proud of is that she has acquired a lot of things, but not one of those things defines her. She doesn't feel that she is defined by dollars. She would be doing what she does even if she wasn't getting paid much. She was just as excited about her first broadcast job making $100 per week as she is about what she does now. Experience and some heartache has taught Oprah that money buys convenience and conveniences. She doesn't knock it but also understands and believes that life's true meaning is about the time you spend with your mate and yourself.[xiii]

Many believe that Oprah's success is attributed to luck and when she was asked, she is quoted as replying, "Luck is a matter of preparation meeting opportunity." I believe Oprah has the right mentality about deserving money, success, and fame. With the right view point, you open yourself up to achieve more of what you believe. If Oprah did not believe she deserved all that she has now, I wonder how much she would have. Certainly she would be successful, but we all know the power of self-sabotage and beliefs.

my story

Why is it that women have a hard time believing we deserve more or even our fair share? I believe it is ingrained in us from an early age. Women have always been maternalistic giving creatures. Wanting to give and give to see pleasure in other's eyes and joy in other's lives.

However, at the end of the day we have difficulty believing we deserve our fair share. That would be rude, inconsiderate and overstepping bounds to ask for more. Often it is more comfortable to stay in one spot and continue with things rather than rock the boat.

I have spoken with thousands of women that have this same issue. It's not that they don't want more, they do. Yet they are not sure that they have worked hard enough, worked long enough or are qualified to deserve more.

Growing up in a small town, we learned to live with less and be happy with it. I personally have had to work hard to shift my own mindset. For many years I saw how hard I was working but couldn't figure out why I wasn't making more. Yet at the end of the day I was forgoing my raise to hire another person or give someone else a raise because I knew they were a single parent and needed it more than me. That's what I felt so I continued to give and give and did not believe that I deserved more myself. All the time I questioned why my hard work wasn't paying off financially for myself.

When I first watched the movie The Secret and then read the book, it hit me like a bolt of lightning. I started journaling feverishly to get to the root cause of my "deserving issue." The more I journaled, the more came flooding out of my head. For years I fell into the trap of not believing that I deserved more than those around me so I did not fight for it or give it to myself.

As I journaled, I realized that I do deserve it. For me, it means money, success, accomplishment, acknowledgement and all the things that come along with each of these. I also realized that my giving nature would be fueled greatly if I shifted my mind set. The more money I can make the more I can give and the greater impact I can leave in this world.

Contrary to what many of us were taught, money is not the root of all evil. It helps many people do many good things if their hearts are in the right place. I have always known my heart is in the right place so now I am focused on making my dreams come true. I stand up for what I deserve in this world and I am not ashamed of that, I am actually proud. Because deep down, I believe I deserve more.

That sounds so simple and appears that this level of confidence came to me over night. Quite the opposite in fact. I have journaled for over three years consistently to get my brain re-wired. To recognize and appreciate the gifts and talents I have been given. To express gratitude to myself for accomplishing all that I have achieved in my seemingly short life.

I have worked diligently to get my mind so focused on abundance and prosperity that when I hear people talk about how they want to make more or deserve more, I have empathy. It is a difficult space to be in and an even harder place to get out of. Yet once you have broken through the barriers, it is absolutely utopia on the other side.

The thoughts and feelings that we have associated with money are usually directly tied to how we were raised as children. If we appreciate money, respect money, mis-manage money or believe money is the root of all evil, each belief usually stems from a childhood association.

When we become adults, the world around us tends to measure all aspects of success and social status by money. However, I believe that it is not all about money. Money is only one component. You must measure your wealth and this encompasses several accounts and money is only one account. For me, I do not obsess with money rather I focus on building true wealth because I know that when I am wealthy, I will have and will be all that I can be.

Here's how I tell people to measure wealth. You have the following accounts in life:

1) Happiness
2) Health
3) Relationships
4) Money
5) Spirituality

At any given time, you merely measure the accounts you have and assess the level of wealth you have. For example, if I have an abundance in the relationship account but my money account is low then I can look towards the relationships I have to help me grow my money account. Or if my money account is overflowing and my health account is low then I have the means to purchase the right tools to improve my health account. If your spirituality account is overflowing but your relationship account is low then determine how you can focus spiritual energy toward increasing your relationship account.

In life there is a balance and when people say, "Money doesn't buy happiness." In the scenario I outlined above, it can actually be used to build the happiness account if there is a deficit. The point is to use excess in one account to build another account until you have an abundance of wealth and all accounts are overflowing. At that point you will have achieved optimal performance and will reap the rewards.

Just as you balance your check book, balance your wealth accounts and you will be truly wealthy in life.

Please work hard to get yourself to utopia and trust me when I say it is heavenly. I live an abundant and joyful life. Each day I am blessed with new gifts and new connections that make my journey in life even more special and unique. You deserve more. You are worth more and it is time that you do what Ginger Rogers did and stand up for yourself. Oprah is one of the largest icons in the world for women, and she doesn't have a problem believing that she deserves great things. She has also set a tremendous example of how having more allows you to give more. What are you waiting for...don't you want to know what's on the other side in utopia? You deserve it.

Success Tip: Are you deserving? Start believing that you deserve all the success you can attract. Before you know it, you'll start seeing positive results via your positive thoughts.

6

Become a Raging River – Fear can be Extremely Powerful

"Willing to do what the average person is not willing to do."
— *Anonymous*

ginger rogers

It was 1930 prior to many of Ginger's musicals, Ginger's mother told her that Florenz Ziegfeld was producing a new movie with Al Jolson and they were looking for a leading lady. Eddie Cantor didn't know Ginger but he took a chance on her and wanted to help so he paved the way for her to audition for this tremendous opportunity.

Ginger was told where to report and when for the initial meeting. In order to get to Mr. Ziegfeld's office, Ginger and her mother had to take a private elevator to the executive area of the Ziegfeld Theater. It was an office that reeked elegance and sophistication. As Ginger and her mother tried to make themselves comfortable, Eddie Cantor bounded into the office with a boyish grin on his face.

His face was gleaming as he explained that he had paved the way and Mr. Ziegfeld had agreed to a private audition right there. Ginger was swallowing hard as Eddie assured her and comforted her letting her know that he would be right there by her side.

The time had come, Ginger and her mother were ushered into the most handsome office with Mr. Ziegfeld standing astutely in the middle of the room. He piped up and said, "Eddie has told me all about you, young lady. As soon as the pianist arrives we will begin."

They all chatted politely until the pianist arrived. As the pianist entered the room, Ginger handed him her music and they began to take their positions. There was a nod and Ginger began singing. Half way through her number, the telephone in the office rang. Mr. Ziegfeld picked up the phone, listened and then hung up that phone and as he reached for another phone, he politely apologized and indicated that he had to take this particular call.

Ginger overheard the conversation and figured out that he was speaking to Al Jolson, the man that Ginger hoped to play opposite in this production. It sounded like he had a woman that he wanted to audition for the role as well. Ginger figured that it was probably his girlfriend at that time. Ginger didn't let this bother her. She finished the audition and received raving compliments from Ziegfeld and Eddie Cantor.

As Eddie was escorting Ginger and her mother out of the offices, he raved about Ziegfeld's comments and then continued. "Ginger, you couldn't begin to guess what the telephone call was all about…the unfortunate thing is that Al Jolson just told Ziegfeld that he has the girl to play his opposite in the movie. And, I'm afraid that's it. There is no discussion since it came directly from Al Jolson, the leading man," said Eddie.

He politely hailed a taxi as Ginger and her mother stood on the sidewalk rather stunned that she had delivered an outstanding audition and it didn't even matter. With one phone call, it was all gone.

As Ginger and her mother got into the taxi cab, Eddie looked at them and said, "Well, Ginger I'm sorry that it didn't work out. But I'm telling you right here, you'll have another show very soon that will give you the opportunity to show your talent. I'm bettin' on you!" He closed the taxi door and they drove off.

Ginger learned another valuable show business lesson that day. As disappointing as it was to lose out, at least she knew that her defeat had nothing to do with her talent. She viewed this merely as an obstacle that she was not going to let stand in her way or stop her. She would figure out a way to work around this, keep going and move onto the next audition. She was not deterred even though she was extremely disappointed.[xiv]

barbara walters

Barbara Walters has said that she feels her entire life has been one big audition. It was not just ambition that drove her. It was not only the desire to prove that she could be something. It was deeper than that. She watched her father rise and fall numerous times.

When she was a child, he was forced to close his agency because he couldn't pay the rent. Then when Barbara was five or six, he had mini-success. Having always been in the entertainment industry, he became a nightclub producer. His success was short-lived as he felt the lingering effects of the great depression. He started touring to make ends meet. Her mother and father were complete opposites. Barbara refers to her mother as the practical one and her father as the one who chose to read poetry, lived in his head and had a difficult time showing affection. He had not graduated from high school but he could certainly quote Shakespeare and knew stories about the Greek Gods.

Barbara watched her father always play it big. Sometimes it worked and sometimes it didn't. Barbara remembered one instance where he took a gamble and moved the entire family from Chicago to Miami. He opened his first night club in Miami Beach late 1940. This was a large gamble yet this became one of the great hit stories for her father. His club became such a success that he was able to hire such talent as Milton Berle, Martha Raye and Sophie Tucker. At first he wasn't sure he could afford such talent, but he made it work. The club became the hot spot for vacationers and his show was bright, happy, sexy and glamorous.

Her father had played big and was successful, which meant her parents were happy and joyful. Barbara had fond memories of this time in her life even though she was a shy and introverted child. She had a difficult time adjusting to new schools and coped by overachieving. She was reading more than was required and doing more homework than was assigned.

One of the key lessons that Barbara learned while in Miami was that the celebrities her father had on stage were real people off stage. She got to know many of them and this served her well later in life. She had an understanding of celebrities that many do not. Because of this real approach to the people, she was not in awe in her later years when she began to interview super stars, high profile actors and dignitaries.

The club was such a success that her father got an itching to move on again. He was ready to find a new challenge and so he did in New York City. It was a tremendous risk that Barbara's mother did not agree with. She was content to continue with what had been working in Miami. But Barbara's father was not and so the family moved yet again.

Her mother was fearful of driving a car. She learned because she had to in order to take Barbara to her orthodontist appointments. Once her braces were removed, her mother quit driving. Her mother was afraid to drive, fearful that someone would hit her. Barbara drove a car briefly after college and otherwise has always had a driver because she was afraid of driving. She even admits to being a terrible back seat driver to this day. Barbara's life was filled with fear. It was rooted deep within her and stemmed from her many childhood experiences. This was natural since her mother was always fearful.

After the family moved to New York City, money became an issue again in the family. Barbara's father's productions were extremely expensive costing $75,000 to $80,000 which was a large amount of money in those days. Barbara watched her mother always afraid that the bottom was going to drop out. Afraid the family would not have any money to feed the children and pay the light bill. So she was frugal with every penny while her father was a generous man. Barbara's father was a gambler and a dreamer. Her mother was a realist whom her father considered a pessimist and what was Barbara? A worrier whom both parents considered to be too serious for a young girl.

After college she was able to get past a lot of her fears. She got a job in advertising primarily because of her legs and partly because she was the top stenographer in her class. Barbara believed in using, or should I say, exposing her assets and nice legs she had. This job only lasted about a year before Barbara was ready to move on. She enlisted her friend to help her get a job with a television station in the publicity department. Barbara had never mentioned her father when interviewing, but this was one time when using her father's name and his celebrity contacts helped her.

At this job Barbara was able to leverage all of her younger years watching her father in the entertainment industry. In the publicity department, columnists would take her calls because she knew how to spin things, she knew what they were looking for and she was in her element. This break and fearless approach in television is what set Barbara on her way. I'm not sure if she ever eliminated all of her fears. But I do know that she eliminated enough fears to become extremely successful in television. Not a lot of people can say that.

Barbara Walters had numerous rocks and boulders placed in front of her and yet she went over them, around them or through them. She became a raging river determined to succeed no matter what stood in her way.[xv]

my story

I believe I have been a raging river all of my life I just didn't know what it was called. I worked when I was twelve washing dishes to pay for the "cool" school clothes I wanted. I worked my way through undergrad and graduate school. Sometimes washing my clothes in the bathtub and walking when I didn't have gas money for my car. When I first started my advertising agency I only had $5,000 dollars in the bank and that went quickly. When it was gone, I found myself doing data entry jobs from my home office just to pay the electric bill. Yet I have always been determined to keep going, doing, and figuring out a way over, under, or through each situation. And that I did.

Then even when the agency was established there were still pockets of time when I struggled to make payroll and wasn't sure how I was going to pay rent. Yet I always figured out a way to make it all work. After all I couldn't let down my team and their families that depended upon them for food and support.

My river slowed as I approached my COD. It was such a difficult physical time that I didn't have the energy to fight as hard as I normally would. I let things go by the way side because I physically just couldn't fight the battle.

After I survived my COD and found my true passion in life, my river has become a raging force to be reckoned with. Now I am more determined than ever in my life to accomplish my goals. I am healthy again and have boundless energy so I know without a doubt that I can go over, under or around any rock that is placed in front of me. When you know deep down that you are unstoppable, you radiate an energy that causes people to stop and take note. They may not know why they are stopped dead in their tracks, but they are and they usually don't ask questions.

Are you a raging river that is unstoppable? Or are you a light brook that is barely flowing and when you reach a rock, you stop? Become a raging river. One that has white caps and moves with such force, people don't dare challenge it or try to stop it. Don't worry about having enough energy to fight for everything you want. Just align yourself and stay balanced. When you are in complete alignment, balanced, and doing what you are passionate about you will have boundless energy that will act as a fuel for your river.

Success Tip: It's up to you and no one ever said succeeding in this world is easy. In fact, most things that are worth it in life are not achieved easily. Become that unstoppable raging river that has an unrelenting determination to accomplish everything you set out to achieve.

7

FINANCIAL FREEDOM CAN BE FOUND IN A BUMBLE BEE

"Starting out to make money is the greatest mistake in life. Do what you have a flair for doing and if you are good enough at it, the money will come."

— *Greer Garson, Actress*

ginger rogers

Ginger Rogers made a career of doing what she was passionate about. Ginger remembered when RKO Studios named a new head of production and bought the property rights to Gay Divorce. He thought the film would be ideal for Fred and Ginger.

At the time, Ginger heard through the grapevine that Fred was not happy with their proposal. He made it clear that he did not want to be associated with one woman for fear that he would be identified with her. Ginger could sympathize with his feelings, but she on the other hand had no apprehensions about making more films with Fred. Primarily because she was constantly appearing in non-musicals without him. For every film that she did with Fred, she was doing three to four without him.

The partnership limitations were only on Fred's part. She technically didn't need him for her career or for the financial rewards that she had been reaping for many years. Unfortunately, Fred was not in the same position as Ginger. He was known primarily as a musical comedy star. Fred finally did agree to make this film with Ginger and the box office proved what the production company had believed, that Fred and Ginger were a hit.

It is interesting to understand that Ginger had already achieved her financial freedom by doing what she loved to do before Fred ever entered into the picture. So often people believe that her financial freedom was because of Fred when in fact, his financial freedom may be directly attributed to Ginger. How ironic that her bumble bee, her passion, made him a wealthy man. That is just my opinion and my view through a modern pair of eye glasses.[xvi]

mary kay

Mary Kay Wagner was born in 1915 or so and her family relocated to Houston when she was a young child. When Mary Kay entered school, she excelled. When Mary Kay graduated, unlike her friends, Mary Kay's family could not afford college so she watched her friends head off to Rice University and she started to look for a job and a husband. Smart she was but forced to face reality. In the 1930's it was easier to find a husband than a job given the conditions brought on by the Great Depression.

She married a singer that she later described as Elvis-like. However, his success was short lived. He lost his radio show and times were tough because the family still needed to eat. They found a job together selling pots and pans. They figured that everyone still needed to eat so this was something in demand and a job they could work together.

They arranged events where Mary Kay would cook dinner in a stranger's kitchen while her husband was in the other room selling the benefits of the pots, pans and pressure cookers. She prepared the same delicious menu every time and when there was leftovers they took them home and had a meal. Quite a meal it was too. Certainly food that they could not afford to eat everyday.

Despite their efforts, there weren't enough people that could afford to purchase new cookware at that time. Mary Kay then found a secretarial job at a local church while her husband went off to war. She didn't make much money, but the $125 per month was more than she had before.

When her husband returned home, she thought it would be a joyous time but was shocked when he told her he wanted a divorce. Mary Kay was devastated. She felt like a complete failure and it was one of the lowest moments in her life. In the midst of being lost and down-trodden, she knew that she needed to find additional work. There was no other option, she didn't have a choice. She had to get up and keep going. Mary Kay started selling home cleaning products for the Stanley Home Products company. She found herself yet again in stranger's homes only this time she was throwing dirt on the floor and hawking mops and other cleaning supplies.

She was good yet she knew that she could improve her sales if she honed her skills. So she started looking for tools and educational resources. Eager to learn, she attended Stanley's regional conference in Dallas. She not only found the knowledge she was seeking but she also found inspiration. The culmination of the meeting was the Crowning of the Sales Queen. Mary Kay watched in awe with the production and all the fuss everyone made. She then proudly told the company's president that she would win that award the following year. He was gracious and looked her straight in the eye and said, "Somehow, I think you will."

Those were the five words that changed her life. She was dedicated and committed to implement what she had learned. She not only increased her sales but she also started working on building a strong downline. She built her organization to a point where she had representatives underneath of her. She was building a strong and lucrative organization that topped 150 people. Stanley was so impressed with her growth and dedication that they asked her to move to Dallas and beef up the efforts there. Viewing this as a tremendous opportunity, she didn't hesitate. She moved from Houston to Dallas and hit the ground running.

She was quickly stopped in her tracks when the company informed her that she would no longer be able to reap the rewards of the downline she had built in Houston. She fought and fought but could not change the minds of those at the corporate office. They were dead set against making an exception. It was discouraging for her because she had spent countless hours and tireless days building that organization and all her hard work was financially for not.

One evening in the 1950's when Mary Kay was showing her cleaning products in yet another stranger's home, she noticed how youthful and smooth the twenty women's faces were. Intrigued, Mary Kay inquired and was told that every woman was using the special emollient sold by the hostess. Curious, Mary Kay inquired and the hostess gave her some product to take home. Mary Kay began applying the product line. Almost immediately, she and her new husband, Richard, noticed a more youthful and glowing face.

Time passed and Mary Kay discouraged and frustrated with the Stanley company. She was tired of watching all the people around her get promoted and reaping the benefits of her hard work in building a strong network. So, she quit.

Sitting in her living room she found herself depressed and feeling lost. In retrospect, she had spent more than twenty-five years peddling products in strangers' homes. As she rubbed her face and looked out the window she found herself staring at the local mortuary. As she continued to rub her forehead she thought how easier it would be if she just called and told them to come pick her up.

As she kept rubbing, inspiration struck her. She realized how smooth and soft her skin was. She also knew how much she had learned about direct sales over the last twenty-five years. She had a brilliant idea. She gathered her sons and her husband around the kitchen table. They were excellent with finances. She mapped out the strategy. The family had saved $5,000 and she proposed that the family invest that in purchasing the rights to the facial emollient formula that she had been using for so long. Then she recommended they secure an office with some basic furniture.

The family was committed to help and support Mary Kay in any way they could. The family decided to commit the entire savings to her new venture. She immediately went out and secured two sales reps and purchased the rights to the formula. They were in business. One morning as they sat at the kitchen table counting their Beauty by Mary Kay sample jars, Richard, Mary Kay's husband, clutched his chest and died from a massive heart attack.

What would Mary Kay do? She buried her husband and then pondered the next steps with her sons. She felt defeated, sad and lonely. She also consulted with their attorney and he was quick to tell her to cut her losses. He assured her that no woman could continue and build a successful company.

She sat at the table with her sons and evaluated her options. One option, she could morn her husband and cash out what she could. With this option in four weeks time she would have little money and would still be morning her husband. The other option was to finish what she had started and reinvent her self.

Her son looked at her and eagerly passed his savings book to his mom. He had $4,500 in the bank and wanted to give it all to her. Her other son was working for an insurance company and immediately said that he would quit his job to work for his mother full time.

Mary Kay was quick to explain that she couldn't pay what he was making with the insurance company. In fact it would be a fraction of that. But her son didn't care. He was committed to helping his mother build her dream. Over the next few months, the accountants and lawyers continued to explain to Mary Kay why her business would fail and how she was going to lose not only her initial investment of $5,000 but also her son's investment of $4,500.

What they didn't count on was her tenacity, persistence and most importantly her passion. Over the first few months in business, she had to face it. It wasn't a wild success. But knowing that she could fix anything, Mary Kay started looking at all of the mistakes she had made and started correcting them one at a time.

To take it to the next level, she knew she needed to go to the roots of her company. She had a high quality product, but more importantly was the reason she was in business and selling her product. It was the passion behind the organization. You see bumble bees technically should not be able to fly because their bodies are too large for their wings. Yet they do fly. She was no different. Mary Kay was on a mission to empower normal housewives that had been told they could not and would not be successful. She wanted to let them fly. With the right product, the right program and the right support these bumble bees could fly. She knew it. She wanted to give them something that she hadn't been given in all her years in the business world: encouragement, empowerment and support. With this she knew that she could make a positive impact on a lot of women's lives.

After following her passion and holding true to her commitment, by the early 1980's she was able to boast that her company had more women earning over $50,000 than any other company in the United States. Today Mary Kay is a multi-billion dollar business. She did not listen to the naysayers. She held true to her passion. Her financial freedom was truly found in a humble bee.[xvii]

my story

What happens when you think you are doing what you are passionate about, yet you really aren't? How do you know? For me, I thought I as doing what I was passionate about yet when I reached my COD, I realized that I wasn't.

As I started to journal and go through the process of finding myself, I realized that there are various levels in which we operate. I deem these the surface, the heart and the gut. When a person is only operating on the surface, they are doing things and pretending that they love what they do. When I refer to the surface I tell people to take their right hand and put it on their left shoulder then drag it across their shoulder bones to the right. It is merely surface. When you operate at this level you are wobbly and not solid.
It is superficial. For me, I had spent several years pretending that everything was great. I had a strong wall built up around me and I was determined not to express vulnerability. I was not going to show emotion and I was going to maintain the image that I thought would generate the greatest results.

As I journaled, I started to tap into the next level, the heart. I realized that people will do things they feel good about. They will often have a heart and compassion for what they are doing. However, this is an emotional level. This is what you reach once you break past the surface. This is at the heart, the center of your chest. Many people believe that operating from the heart is perfectly fine. However, I believe there is a significant difference once you pass from there to your gut, which is the true passion point.

Wondering what I am referring to? Let me explain. Have you ever been in a situation where you saw someone slam their hand on a table and express emotion about the topic at hand? That's operating from the heart. When you move beyond that and reach your gut, your passion point, you are at the optimal level for performance and financial freedom.

When someone is operating at this level, you may see them slam their fist on the table but there isn't emotion in their statement, there is conviction. A big difference and when you see it, you feel it and you know it. That is the optimal level that you want to achieve so that you are unleashing your bumble bee to fly.

After a long time of journaling, I found my passion. It is helping other entrepreneurs become successful, women entrepreneurs in particular. What I found in the process I went through was that marketing was not my passion. Which was a shock since I had been successful in marketing for nearly 20 years. It is instead my gift. I have been blessed with that gift in life and now I use it as a tool to help me live my passion.

I suggest that you sit down and take a hard look at what you are doing. What level are you operating at? Are you merely on the surface pretending that everything's alright? Are you denying your own self of the truth? Are you operating purely from an emotional state and not from the gut? When you examine the levels within yourself, it is like peeling away the layers of an onion. You will feel exposed and you may shed a few tears but you will get to the center.

When you get to your gut level, the true passion level there will be no stopping you. People that operate in this realm equate it to having a fire in your belly. There isn't anything that will stand in your way. You operate from a level of conviction that few can understand.

In this process, many people are afraid. Afraid of what this will feel like. Afraid of being too exposed and vulnerable. Yet this is the beauty of operating at this level. You are vulnerable. You are exposed yet you believe with such conviction that you are virtually unstoppable. You will emit the energy levels that will attract what you need when you need it.

Now that I operate solely at the passion level, my life is unbelievable. It is utopia. I feel great mentally and physically. I am attracting what I need as I need it. I am also attracting what I want when I want it. There is a significant difference and it is nice to be in such a focused state of mind.

I can only imagine that this is the state of mind that Mary Kay operated in for so many years. How rewarding it must have been knowing that she was impacting positively the lives of women around the world. I pale in comparison and merely strive to achieve a fraction of the satisfaction that she experienced.

Success Tip: Are you ready to find your financial freedom? If you find your passion, you will fly. Despite what all the naysayers tell you, you can fly. Even if they are the supposed experts just remember that supposed experts said bumble bees shouldn't fly and these experts were clearly wrong.

8

POWER – FIND YOURS AND EMBRACE IT

"What I wanted to be when I grew up was in charge."
— *Brigadier General Wilma Wright*

ginger rogers

Ginger Rogers was reluctant to ask for what she wanted. In part she said it was because she was shy. But also because she had become so reliant on others around her like her mother and other professionals. This hindered her for years. She found herself accepting parts that were not always flattering to her talents and abilities. She also believed that she was worth more than what she was getting paid. Yet hadn't discovered the power of her voice at that time to demand more. She would simply acquiesce and she did that for years.

Finally in 1936, as she and her agent were negotiating a new contract with RKO Studios, Ginger finally had mustered up the courage to ask for what was rightfully hers. She wanted not only more money but also roles that were more well suited for her. You see by contract, she was not able to refuse the films she was being given. Also before the Screen Actors Guild was formed, actors could be kept working until they fell down on their face. Actors were often strained from lack of rest which Ginger constantly fought herself.

Not once was Ginger absent from the set. Many other actresses would take two or three days off for that certain time of the month. They did that every month. Not Ginger. She never missed a day. Her films were making big money for the studios and she finally found her internal power to stand up and ask for what was rightfully hers. For all of those years, she had allowed herself to miss out on the financial rewards by not making any demands.

She had found her power voice and was unleashing it. She drew a line in the sand and said that she would not arrive at the studio until something was done about her contract. Finally, when the big studio brass realized that Ginger was not kidding, they re-considered and negotiated her contract. While they were drafting a new contract, Ginger still refused to go on set. She would not arrive until the new contract was agreed upon and signed. She rightfully stood her ground and won. She found her internal power and from that day forward, she negotiated each and every contract.

She no longer took a back seat and allowed things to continue status queue. She would never again allow someone to stifle her internal power and deprive her of what was rightfully hers. After all, she was still making significantly less than Fred Astaire even though she was more seasoned and worked twice as many hours.

Internal power is interesting because it can remain dormant for an extended period of time but once it is unleashed, there is no turning back. The power will never be stifled again, just as with Ginger so it is with every woman.[xviii]

hillary clinton

Look at Hillary Clinton. She arrived at Yale in the fall of 1969 and was one of 27 women among the total law student population of 235. She stepped on campus bringing with her a reputation for being a bold leader and an activist. She had spent her years at Wellesley making a bold statement and that quickly set the tone for her at Yale.

Students viewed her as a leader already. They believed that she was destined for electoral politics and that she had chosen Yale as the school to catapult her career. One of her female class mates said, "Hillary knew she wanted to be politically influential and prominent. She wanted recognition."

Hillary found her internal power and has harnessed that over the years. She developed a successful legal career and then assumed a supportive role as then Governor Bill Clinton took office. A woman many believe has a strong sense of balance, poise and sophistication, she also exuded a sense of true self control and inner power. When President Clinton took office, many people believed that she was overly involved with her political role. I believe the contrary. In my opinion, she was the first First Lady to assume a more prominent and active role. She was demonstrating her personal power to try and achieve movement in the health care industry. Whether you believe in her position or not, to me it was apparent that she was wielding more personal power than any other First Lady in history.

Even though public opinions have varied over the years, I was excited to see her run for President of the United States. I thought it was a courageous move and one that took great poise, skill and tremendous discipline of her personal power. She is a leader that we can learn from as women because she has lived most of her adult life in the public's eye. A position that requires significantly more self-control and strategic planning than many of us will ever experience in our lifetime. I admire her and strive to have as much personal power as she does.[xix]

queen elizabeth

Queen Elizabeth has been referred to as the greatest monarch ever to rule England. She was a true leader that has significant historical importance. She came from a dysfunctional family and operated in a barely functioning world. Elizabeth was crowned in 1558 when England was a victim of itself and of its competitors. When Elizabeth died in 1603, after reigning for forty-five years, England was the richest and most powerful nation in Europe and was well on its way to becoming the greatest empire the world would ever know, according to many.

Elizabeth has been referred to as one of the greatest leaders in history. She obviously had power but how did she develop it? How did she use it in a time when a woman's place was clearly not typically in this type of leadership position. In fact, most people during that time believed that women were not only intellectually and temperamentally unsuited to be in a leadership position but morally incapable as well.

She had internal power from an early age and in her leadership role was able to easily adapt. Elizabeth did not act suddenly or sweepingly. She handled her position with a combination of prudence, boldness and genius. She had great restraint and decisive patience. She was able to effect change slowly and in ways that would allow enough of the old to be preserved that it gave people more comfort in handling the change. She did not act alone. She had a talented team of people around her.

She also understood the value of image. Most powerful women know that how they portray themselves either helps or hinders them in a powerful position. For her, she realized that the image that would best suite her situation was the feminine ideal of the virgin who was pale, fair of hair and of a willowy ethereal figure.

She was true to this image and spent a great deal of time ensuring her face was powdery white, the pupils of her eyes were almost always dilated which made a more stark contrast between her black eyes and her pale white skin, and she found just the right mixture of berries to highlight her lips a crimson red. All in an effort to ensure the image she held was true to the image her people would respect most as a powerful female leader.

As a powerful leader, she was never ashamed to speak and present her mind. She spent a significant amount of time ensuring that her mind was sound and that she always operated with the proper principles. Because she had prepared her internal self, she was able to outwardly present her mind in such a fashion that would be respected by those around her. With this type of internal foundation, she was able to communicate with confidence and present her own mind with greater ease.

She demonstrated the ultimate of power. She was able to keep her head, make wise decisions and command the respect of those around her. All at a time when women were not thought of as capable of having intelligence let alone a leadership position such as this.

How did she manage her power on a daily basis? What were the tools and tips that women today can learn from? There were some basics that she followed. First, she framed her request as a request, not a demand. This is a trait that is found in many persuasive people. They never impose upon someone else. Instead they present their point of view in such a fashion that it becomes the point of view of the other person.

Secondly, Elizabeth proposed positive action. She did not want to punish those who spread rumors. Rather she wanted to stop the rumors. She knew that punishment was a negative action that did not address the true root of the issue. She believed that negative action would only intensify the evil will of the people. Positive energy and a positive force would address the root of the problem by stopping rumors before they were even started.

Thirdly, Elizabeth proposed action by someone else. She believed that it was far more effective to have someone else toot her horn than to toot it herself. A concept that proves valid even today. It has a far greater impact to have someone else sing your praises than to hear someone sing their own praises. She believed that she could defend herself against gossip, but it was far more effective to have others declare the gossip untrue.

Fourthly, she appealed to the good beyond herself. Many of us, especially women, are not comfortable asking for favors. Elizabeth appealed to people to help her do greater good and be part of something much larger. That's how she motivated those around her to step up, make a commitment and give what she needed to have given.

Elizabeth also believed that intellect was a gift but learning was hard work. She was a voracious reader and tried to learn everything she could. This was a trait that she adopted at an early age. She wanted to fashion herself into an enlightened leader.

With her inner beliefs solid, she was able to handle the situations that arose with dignity and poise. Even when faced with extremely difficult and challenging situations, she never panicked. She knew that by panicking, she would concede to being powerless in any given situation. She knew that by remaining calm, she could rationally think through a situation and ensure that she exploited it to the fullest potential or diminish it. Either way, by not panicking, she was able to control the situation and create the desired outcome.

Elizabeth wielded tremendous power and was able to accomplish a significant amount during her reign. What I admire most about her is the resolve she had. When a woman has resolve and is confident and grounded in her beliefs, she can unleash her own power and she will be able to accomplish greatness. It is when there is no internal foundation that a woman's power is misinterpreted, misunderstood and not deemed appropriate.

If a Queen that reigned nearly 500 years ago can accomplish all that she did, then women today can stand up, build an internal foundation and unleash their power within.[xxi]

my story

For years I denied the true power that I have within me. I stifled it and suppressed it. Only let out what I thought I needed in order to excel in my career. Looking back it is amazing that I would have done that. I am one who always holds true to my core. Yet deep down I believe that I was afraid to embrace my true power. I was afraid to lose friends. I was afraid of how I would be perceived. If I let it out, would people think I was a power hungry witch? I wouldn't want that. If I let it out, what success would I achieve and what would that mean? How would my life change?

Bottom line it was fear of the unknown. Fear and uncertainty of what I would face, what it would mean and how it would make me feel. I remember my first job out of college. I worked for the largest hotel management company in the world and they were headquartered in Denver, Colorado.

At that time the hotel industry was certainly a good 'ole boys club. This company was no exception. I was hired as a marketing coordinator and I worked on the fourteenth floor. All of the women on that floor were "secretaries" except for me and two other women. I do mean secretaries, not administrative assistants. Of the three of us not in that category, one woman was a vice president and the other was one of the corporate attorneys.

The vice president was nearly six feet tall and slender. She carried herself with grace, dignity and distinction. I could see how she had inner power. Yet I also saw how she was treated. The men did not treat her as an equal and did not respect her level of power.

The legal counsel was a cold woman that was extremely harsh and difficult. She had a tall wall built up around her and she had no intention of letting it down. She had respect purely because she did not break the mold. She never smiled, always had her lips pursed and was difficult to work with. Everyone knew it. I never saw or felt a true power in her. It was power through title, I believe.

That was my first experience in watching how women's power was respected, received and embraced. I was the only woman in the business development department, except for one "secretary" named Beth. I figured out early on that I could learn a lot from those around me. So I became a sponge. I wasn't worried about power in those days. I didn't have enough experience to even think of having power. I just tried my best to learn the inner workings, watch the politics and try to figure out how the business worked.

When I was in my review, it was apparent how the business worked. I was told that in order to move up in the department, I would have to work in every type of hotel that the company managed. From limited service to full-service to suburban to boutique to resort. Then and only then would it be possible for me to gain a promotion.

Today, I would have stood my ground and created a new position. I would have prepared my case as to why the company needed the new position and why I was the best candidate. But I think that's what age and experience brings. Chutzpah is what most people call it.

At that time, I said yes and I was transferred out to a hotel in the sales department. I listened to what they said literally and worked in every type of hotel. I was on a mission to gain the experience faster than anyone else. I changed jobs every six months for a promotion to a better title, better pay and one step closer to the corporate position I wanted.

When I landed at a suburban hotel as the national sales manager, I was in for a real treat. I exceeded my goals, made my bonus, and was given a new territory. One that didn't exist and I built it from scratch. I knew the inner workings. How to balance room rates and occupancy based upon day of the week and time of the year. I could motivate staff and keep people from complaining. One day when the director of sales resigned, I thought I had my chance. I had been doing her job for the most part anyway. The only thing I had not been doing each day was the reports for the general manager. I was thrilled because I thought it was my chance to really shine, step up and show what I was made of.

The general manager approached me one morning and asked that in the interim if I would step into that role and assume the responsibilities. I gladly said yes. I didn't even ask for more money, ask what the plan was or anything. I just said yes. Again, hind site is certainly 20/20. Today I would have said, "What's the game plan for this position? Are you interviewing candidates from the outside and inside? What is the time frame to fill the slot? What do you expect from me in this interim fill in? Will I be considered for the position?" But at that time, I didn't even think of those questions. I was too naïve and inexperienced in the ways of the world.

I thought that if I stepped into that position I could prove my power and show that I could do a good job. Unfortunately, that was not the case. A month later, the general manager came back to me. I had been moved into the director of sales office and had assumed the duties just as he asked. I was completing reports, managing the team all while still exceeding the quota of my old position. He sat across from me and had the nerve to ask me to train the new director of sales. She would start on Monday and he wanted to make sure that I could ensure she was brought up to speed and well trained.

Yes, train my new boss. If I could do the job so well that I could train my new boss, then why wasn't I the boss? That's the question I asked. Apparently there was an unwritten rule somewhere in the hotel industry that said a person had to be forty years old before he or she could become a director of sales. I was twenty four years old at the time. I obviously was qualified to do the job because I had filled in for a month and was asked to train the new person.

I look at that situation now as a perfect example of how a woman needs to embrace and appreciate the power she has within her. I knew inside of me that I could have a positive impact on that hotel. I could do that job better than the replacement coming in the door. I knew it deep down. But I had not conveyed my inner power in a manner that would convince them to take a chance on a younger than usual director of sales.

I'm sure you are wanting to know what did? Well, I came in on Monday and I started training the new boss. That was after I turned in my resignation with my two weeks notice. I took a move up to another resort hotel and never looked back.

Power for women is a funny thing. So many of us know deep down that we have it yet we are afraid to let it out. We may sometimes let just enough out to get what we want and then stifle it again. It has come from years of experience, many failures, numerous triumphs and many embarrassing situations that I am now able to embrace my inner power. Part of embracing is realizing the image you portray. If you always cower and shrink yourself when in a situation, then you are not expressing your inner power. Stand tall and push your shoulders back. For me that involves wearing high heels and always having a 2 inch tease in my hair so that on any given day I am nearly 5'8". Yet straight out of the shower I am only…let's just say I love the man who first invented high heels.

That is what works for me so that challenge is to figure out what works for you. What makes you feel most powerful? When are you most empowered? Take notice of what you are wearing, how you are walking and how you are acting. Those are key pieces of information because you will want to duplicate and replicate that in order to achieve lasting impact.

I reflect back on the women that I have worked with over the last twenty years and I often think of those that abused power and those that stifled their power. I never had a role model per se. I turned to national figures to find my role models and know to this day the women I admire the most are some of the most controversial women who have plowed paths where one had not previously existed.

That will be another book for another day. In the mean time, I encourage women to take the first step and at least find their inner power. Then start to embrace it. Get comfortable with it. Most of us have tremendous power and it is actually scary how much power we have. That is until you learn to embrace it and appreciate it. That is easier said than done. It takes time to get comfortable with your own power. Once you do then you can move forward with the confidence you need to let your power shine. Let it out, use it to take you further and help those around you.

Success Tip: The world will be a better place when every woman embraces her own power and honors the great gifts she has been given in this world. We have to start somewhere. Are you ready to find your power? I see that smile on your face. You know you have it in you so start bringing it out and welcome the new adventures you will embark upon.

9

IT'S A GAME

"The trouble with the rat-race is that even if you win, you're still a rat."
— *Lily Tomlin*

ginger rogers

Business is a game and Ginger demonstrated this with great ease many times. But there was one instance where she was absolutely brilliant. She had reached a point where she believed she was pigeon holed with the parts she was being offered and how the industry was viewing her.

At a party one evening, Ginger approached the producer of Mary of Scottland, a new film that the studio was getting ready to film starring Kathryn Hepburn. Ginger wanted the role of Queen Elizabeth and asked specifically that he consider her for that role. The producer, Mr. Berman, was shocked. He could not even begin to think that Ginger Rogers could play that role. He told her, "You should be glad you do what you do so well. Why don't you just stick to your high-heeled slippers and be happy?" As he finished his sentence he gently brushed her off and mingled through the party.

Ginger called her agent, Leland Hayward, and told him that she would be perfect for that role. She begged him to call Mr. Berman and convince him that she would be the right fit for this role. Leland's recommendation to Ginger was to corner the director, John Ford, in the commissary during lunch. He believed that would be a better approach for her and would actually give her a real ear to hear her out.

Ginger thought that was a brilliant idea so she did some digging around and figured out what time Mr. Ford was typically in the commissary for lunch. Then, she had to devise a plan. She realized that if she showed up as Ginger Rogers he would likely not give her the time of day. She thought and then it came to her. If she showed up as Elizabeth, in full character, then Mr. Ford couldn't judge her on being Ginger but would only be able to judge her on the character she wanted to play, Elizabeth.

The stage was set. She called Leland and explained her plan to him. She wanted to show up on set as a British actress named Lady Ainsley. She asked Leland to make the calls that would set the buzz in motion for Lady Ainsley, a British actress that as far as the studio was concerned, might be able to be talked into playing the role of Queen Elizabeth. He made the phone call as Ginger got on the phone with make-up and wardrobe, explained the situation and then made them both swear to secrecy.

The day of the test Ginger spent a significant amount of time in wardrobe and make-up. They made her skin pasty white and her eyes were beady looking and had a narrowness to them. They painted a slit mouth over her lips and she sported a brunette wig. After wardrobe was done with her, she was a true Queen Elizabeth from head to toe. All she had to do was bring it together with her attitude and accent.

Leland phoned John Ford and explained that Lady Ainsley had been playing Shakespearean roles for the past five years in London and that her husband, Lord Ainsley, was on safari so she accepted an invitation to visit the states and stay with Mary Pickford. He went on to say that Lady Ainsley was a huge fan of John Ford's films and that she would also enjoy meeting Katherine Hepburn.

John Ford ate it up. He bought the whole thing hook line and sinker. When the time came, Ginger (I mean Lady Ainsley) strolled on stage and she felt ten feet tall. No one recognized her as Ginger. She passed by several people that were dear friends of hers and each of them bowed. Ginger had a ball fooling all of the folks she had worked with month after month.

John Ford approached her and explained that he was delighted to meet her and that he had seen her perform in London the previous year. Lady Ainsley was cordial and then they moved her to the set for the test. Katherine Hepburn was on stage as Ginger approached and got into position. They said the magic words…lights, camera, action.

The test was complete and everyone cordially thanked Lady Ainsley for taking the time to audition. Ginger left the set and passed by a very dear friend that never flinched. It was amazing to her that no one could recognize her. Everyone said they would get back to her once they watched the test.

A couple of days later, Leland called Ginger and explained that the producer (Mr. Berman) had seen the tests and liked them. He wanted them re-shot with sound. Now her game was really snowballing. Someone leaked the story and the following day, it was the feature of a prominent Hollywood columnist. People called it a practical joke, but what most didn't realize is that the game really wasn't a game because Ginger had her heart set on that part. She was willing to do anything to demonstrate that she could play the part.

When she read the column, Ginger quickly raced to the phone. She had to call Mr. Berman and speak with him before he read the paper. He wasn't home. What should she do? Stay at home and keep trying to phone him or spend the day at the race track with her friend. If she went to the races, she would risk running into Mr. Berman. But, she couldn't just sit at home. She went to the races and made it through the gates. All of a sudden, she heard a voice from behind her saying, "You little devil! You know you really had me going. That was the best trick ever pulled on me. I had no idea that you were that 'lady' I saw on the screen. I never would have guessed it was you!" Thankfully he had a sense of humor and was not angry. Ginger laughed and then suggested that she do a second test for him.

Ginger didn't get the second test and didn't get the part. But to her, she had played the game the way she needed in order to show people that she could do more than dance. It was in the media and people talked. Even though she didn't get the part, she had shown them what she was made of and that she could play their game [xx]

robin roberts

"Many of us are quick to think the worst of people – and to assume they think the worst of us. That's exhausting," said ESPN sportscaster Robin Roberts. She wrote this in her book and then went on to talk about the first time that she came home and complained to her parents that she did not get a job because she was black.

It didn't take long for her mother to look her square in the eyes and say, "Did you stop to think that maybe you didn't get the job because you're not good enough?" That was the truth and that hurt. But it was how Robin was raised and how Robin's mother was raised.

Throughout the years, Robin had her sister who helped guide her and show her the way. It was her sister that opened her eyes to the career that Robin would follow. She explained that Robin loved sports and thoroughly enjoyed broadcasting so why not combine them and become a woman sportscaster. Robin dismissed this notion at first believing that it would not be possible. Then she remembered some of the things that she was taught. She could do anything and there were no barriers, only the barriers you create yourself.

Robin didn't play the games that other people played. She only followed the rules as long as she had to. For example, in sportscasting, her gender was more often a bigger barrier than her race. She knew when she started into sportscasting that it wasn't going to be easy because women sportscasters were few and far between.

In the early 1980's there was a lot of controversy over women in the men's locker rooms. Robin made it clear that she wasn't fighting for equal access to the locker room. She was fighting for equal access to the athlete who just happened to be in the locker room. When Robin went to work in Atlanta for WAGA, she had her first major assignment at the University of Georgia covering the Southeastern Conference Men's Basketball Tournament. This university was like many other universities and they had a policy of no women in the men's locker rooms. They had an interview room and the reporter had to put in a request and then wait for the athlete to enter the interview room.

Robin did this and she sat patiently with her camera man. She wanted to respect the rules and the guidelines that they had set forth. After she watched every one of her competing television male sportscasters walk out of the locker room with their footage, she decided it was not about breaking rules, it was about keeping her job. If she didn't get the interview taped in time for the late night news and every other station had the report, she was certain she would be fired.

She grabbed the camera man and promptly started to march into the locker room. She was stopped at the door by someone from the university and she sternly explained that she wanted an interview with the leading athlete. She must have made quite an impression because within a matter of a few seconds, the athlete was standing in front of her dripping wet. They had literally pulled him out of the shower to come talk to her. At least he had the mindset to grab a towel to cover himself up.

Playing the game means understanding what it takes to get accomplished what needs to be accomplished. In this case, Robin knew what she had to get that night and she went after it. She had played the game up until this point and then went out on a limb to prove herself, and that she did. She is highly regarded in the broadcast field and reached a significant milestone when she was named as one of the co-anchors on the Good Morning America Show with Charlie Gibson and Diane Sawyer.[xxi]

my story

I vividly remember when I started my first job out of college. I worked for Aircoa, which at that time was the largest hotel management company in the world. I was hired as a marketing coordinator in the business development department.

It was certainly a learning experience for me. The first day I arrived on the job, I was the only one of three women on that entire floor to have an office. Every other woman was a secretary. Yes, I mean secretary because at that time they did not call the position administrative assistant.

I was the only woman in the entire department, except for Beth who was Hank's secretary. I traveled across the county and was put in charge of a multi-million dollar department budget. My naïve country bunkin' personality came out quickly in many instances. I didn't know what I didn't know. I did not understand the political games that went on in a large corporation. I learned quickly how to cautiously tip toe around certain aspects and situations.

I learned as much as I could as fast as I could. I was on a mission to grow and be promoted and I didn't want to wait forever either. (My patience level hasn't changed much in the last eighteen years.) I was doing a great job and had the praise of my colleagues and my boss.

I remember sitting in my review with Hank, my boss, and asking what the next promotion level would be and what I needed to do in order to qualify for it. He was quick to respond. He told me that I would not be able to be promoted in that department until I had worked for every type of hotel in the industry. I asked a couple of additional questions and he told me again, "You have to work for a limited service hotel, suburban hotel, resort and convention hotel before you can be promoted." He explained that even though I had been doing the market analysis and research, it would take this firsthand experience in order for me to be promoted.

I listened and started on that path. I was willing to play the game. I set out on a mission but when I was told that I would have to be forty years old before I could be a director of hotel sales, I decided that was enough. I didn't need to play their games in order to get ahead in life. I could make my own way, pave my own path and create my own game.

I think that as women we can usually understand the game and we often respect the game, but realize we don't have to play the game. I must say that I am much wiser now and am keenly aware that everything I do in business and every deal I make involves a game. Not because of me, but because of the way things work.

With this view point, I then analyze and analyze then I create a game plan to win. I am extremely competitive and as my father always said, "Second place still means you lost." I am driven to always win and in each situation I have learned to look at the levels and components that are below the surface. It is this level that will determine if you can succeed or not. It is this level where you understand the rules of the game.

Success Tip: Start looking at every business situation as a game. Look closely for the rules, understand the players, define their motives and then create your game plan. Let's face it, business is a game. The sooner you understand that the sooner you can chose to win, lose or draw.

10

PLAY BIG OR GO HOME

"We don't know who we truly are until we see what we can truly do."
— *Martha Grimes, Author*

ginger rogers

Ginger Rogers learned firsthand from her mother how to play big. In 1915, her mother carried out her threat to go to Hollywood with her idea for a movie. She went armed with nothing more than her talent, her grit and an abiding interest in social reform, in particular with regard to penal code which is what she had focused on for years.

When she arrived in Los Angeles, she quickly discovered that producers were concerned less with penal reform than with finding scripts for their glamorous stars. There was a rumor floating around that scripts were desperately needed for the reigning movie queen of the time, Theda Bara. Ginger's mother, Lela, wasn't that fond of Theda but decided that she could get past that if producers were that desperate for scripts appropriate for her.

Lela attended a party one evening and ran into a film director. Lela asked him if it was in fact true that they were desperate for material for Theda. He confirmed that and Lela told him her idea. She explained the plot for the film and the director encouraged her to put her idea down on paper as he felt it would be a viable script for Theda.

Lela took that encouragement and sat down at her large Underwood typewriter and started banging out page after page until she believed the script was finished. She didn't have past experience in writing scripts, but when she reviewed what she had written, she believed it was good. After all, the director said he thought the idea was good and why would he lie to her.

Lela's script was purchased and filming began with Theda as the star. Lela collected her check and considered herself an official active motion picture writer. Then she saw the film and realized that it barely resembled the script that she sold the studio. Apparently the director changed it, then the producer and so on until the film was made.

It didn't matter to Lela. The point for her was that she had taken a tremendous risk to get herself to Los Angeles and was determined to play in the big leagues. And she did. She made it happen with nothing more than her own innate talent and her drive to succeed.

Lela was a great role model for Ginger as she watched her stretch and continuously play big.[xxii]

estee lauder

I wish that I would have been able to interview Estee Lauder in person. She is the epitome of a woman who played big. A woman so determined that no rock or boulder could stand in the way of her building a billion dollar global cosmetic empire.

She had many obstacles placed in front of her over the years which tested her each and every time. Most businesses are faced with COD but Estee was living in a world of CBD (Cash Before Delivery) she had to pay her vendors. She is quoted as saying that in the early years she cried more than they ate.

Yet she managed to put on her finest dress which most of the time she really couldn't afford but she knew that she had to look the part in order to avoid the NOKD remarks from the socialites. That stands for "not our kind". She managed to dress well enough to pass the snob factor and avoid this dreadful acronym. She knew she had to play big as well as look and act like the "big people."

When Estee decided to take her product to the major market, she set her eyes on Saks Fifth Avenue. She knew that this was the type of store where her product belonged. She would have had an easier time approaching the mid-level stores, yet she was determined to hold true to what she believed...her product was top of the line and belonged in top of the line stores.

She knocked on the doors at Saks and she got no response. Not even from her first phone call to her fiftieth phone call. Estee didn't give up. She looked at this as persistence and she was determined to keep at it until she got a break. And a break she got. It took some good luck which was disguised in the form of bad luck for Estee to get her break. One of the assistant buyers for Saks was scraped up in a car accident. Estee decided to "prescribe" her a special healing regimen that ended up working very well.

The Saks buyer heard of Estee's miracle work and sent her daughter to Estee's home. When Estee answered the door she was faced with a girl sporting a veil. It was not being worn for religious reasons rather to hide the girl's pimpled skin. Estee gave her a formula that not only worked, only it worked extremely well.

Finally after hearing of the astounding results people had achieved from Estee's product, the buyer for Saks finally gave in after Estee's millionth request. They placed an order for $800 in product. It was a small order and Estee knew it, but still determined she knew she could figure out a way to magnify this small order and give it the magnitude and recognition that she deserved.

She was able to persuade the Saks buyer to send out a gold leaf card to all of the charge account holders announcing the proud addition of the Estee Lauder line of cosmetics now available at Saks. Talk about a raging river that would not give up. Estee was ahead of her time indeed. This was four years before an American Express card was even issued and the forerunner to Visa didn't even appear for another twelve years.

This strategy paid off and Saks was sold out of the small order of product within two days. She took this win and hit the road approaching all types of high end retailers. She knew that the one large account she wanted was Neiman Marcus. She called and called and called and each time she was given a new excuse. Wrong time of day, wrong time of month, inventory, wrong time of year and so on. Finally the manager gave in and accepted her call. Estee was proud of her accomplishments with Saks in New York and quickly touted these to the man on the other end of the phone.

Not impressed, he quickly reminded her that Dallas was a long way from Central Park and it didn't matter to him how things were done in New York City because they were darn sure done differently in Dallas, Texas. She was feeling a bit disheartened, but she didn't give up. She kept calling and kept calling. Finally, he gave in and he decided to give her a small amount of counter space the day after New Years. As he was chuckling knowing that was the worst time and certain that Estee would fail, he took comfort that he would have her off his back once and for all.

Estee didn't mind. She hung up the phone and shrieked because she was in Neiman Marcus. Just as she had done with the Saks opportunity in New York, Estee knew she had to make this small accomplishment appear large. She contacted a radio station in Dallas that had a predominantly female listening audience.

She got on the program New Years Day and gave the interview of her life. She said that she was just in from Europe with the latest in beauty tips for women and if they came in to see her the next day, each woman would receive a free gift with purchase. Then she let it roll. The slogan her company used for years was first coined that day in Dallas, "Start the New Year with a new face."

You guessed it. She sold out and was a hit in Dallas. It took her persistence with the manager and determination to make the small victory a milestone for her business. Then she figured since she was telling women in Dallas that she was fresh in from Europe, she might as well expand to Europe.

Yet again, she was not welcomed with open arms. Even with all of the success she had achieved in the United States with prominent high end retailers, European retail buyers were not interested. She approached stores and was repeatedly turned away, snubbed in fact. They would not have her dabbing cream on them after all they had Channel. She did not let this seemingly large obstacle stop her.

She walked into one of the finest stores in Paris and had the gall to do what most of us would never dream of. She "accidentally" spilled her perfumed Youth Dew bath oil on the floor and then watched as the sweet-smelling fragrance enshrouded the shoppers. They loved the scent. Soon French women could buy Youth Dew at the counter rather than just sloshing in it on the floor.[xxiii]

Talk about playing big. Estee believed without a doubt that she was going to make it big. She knew her product was of high quality and that she belonged in the high society circles. I believe that a significant part of her success can be attributed to her unwavering confidence and inner belief.

Do you have that inner belief that you can play big? Or are you scared to play big and ready to go home? Every time you think about "going home" and not playing big, just remember Estee Lauder. If she had gone home we wouldn't have the free gift with purchase. And let's face it we all love our free gift with purchase.

my story

I have been playing big all of my life. I was the youngest of five and there were fifteen years difference between me and my oldest brother. As I look back on my childhood I'm not sure what it was that my parents instilled in me. Perhaps it is a simple lesson that I learned early on. If I behaved like an adult, I would be treated like an adult. As I look back, this probably explains why people always told me I was more mature for my age.

I took full advantage of it too. My parents would let me ditch school to meet with the CPA when they had their taxes prepared. It was only right since I had helped total up the numbers on the calculator and file the checks in specific categories. I felt like I was part of my father's business. I sat in the CPA's office and acted as if I knew exactly what he was saying and understood all the details even though I was only nine years old.

It is this ability to go out on a limb that is a mindset I am grateful for having been raised with. I have been able to use that to my advantage in life. My husband has always told me that if you look the part and act the part then you'll get the part. That certainly worked for me when I was in the corporate world and has also worked for me with my own businesses. If I wanted to work with a celebrity, I knew that I needed to look like a celebrity and act like an experienced celebrity in order to get the business.

When you play big there is always stretching involved. You must stretch until it is uncomfortable then stretch a bit further in order to achieve your potential. I remember sitting in the audience of the national eWomen Network Conference in Dallas, Texas. This was my first time attending and it was the opening night banquet. Just as we finished our dinner they started the live auction benefiting their foundation.

I had my eyes on one of the packages that was being auctioned. It was a CNBC media package that included meeting with Sharon Epperson of CNBC, touring Hearst Publishing and meeting with Donny Deutsch who had the CNBC program, The Big Idea. I knew the value of media exposure and relationships so when they announced this package, I sat straight up in my chair and pulled out my program. The package started at $5,000 and I quickly raised my program as my sign of bidding. I continued to raise my program until it reached $15,000.

I swallowed hard, gulped and tried to maintain my composure because I had a camera in my face and it was projected across three 12-foot screens in the room with 3,000 women watching me. I hesitated because I thought I would only need to spend about $10,000 on the package. I smiled and turned to my right where Rachel was sitting. She simply looked at me and said, "Play big or go home."

I looked at her and smiled even bigger. It was somewhat shocking to me to hear her say that because she had just started as my administrative assistant on Monday and we flew to Dallas on Wednesday. So here she was on day three telling me to play big or go home.

She was right. I thought for a moment and wondered how I could stand in front of crowds of people and tell them that they need to play big if I couldn't even play big. So I raised my program and held my arm in the air. I was determined to win the package. I was also hopeful that the other bidder would give up sooner than later as this was getting to be expensive.

I won the package and paid $30,000. Many people think I am crazy for spending that much money. After all I hadn't budgeted that. It was six months worth of my public relations budget spent at one time on a few days in New York.

Yet I knew it would be worth it. I had two round trip tickets so, of course, Rachel joined me. We spent the afternoon with Sharon Epperson on the floor of the NYMEX and that was October 2008 when the stock market dropped nearly 800 points in one day. It was an unbelievable experience. We had a great conversation with Sharon and gained a strong appreciation of her key role in reporting the business news for CNBC.

The next day we toured Hearst Publishing and then went to the CNBC studios in New Jersey. We spent the entire afternoon there. Touring the facility, all of the sets and meeting behind the scenes people. We spent time in the green room for The Big Idea show and rubbed elbows with the likes of Dan Cathey, CEO of Chick-Fil-A. He is a genuine and nice man who has a great team of people that truly exemplify their company's mission statement.

We watched the taping of the show and then had the opportunity of a lifetime. We sat and met with Donny Deutsch for 30-minutes. What a dream come true for me. I have always admired him and had a tremendous amount of respect for him. After all he had taken his father's advertising agency and infused new life into it. He built it to become one of the leading agencies globally and then sold it for several hundred million dollars.

I was pleased that he is such a gracious and humble man. Many people ask me if I was nervous and if it was hard to start the conversation with Donny? The answer is no. Surprisingly it wasn't. I have enough inner confidence and had done enough research on him that I felt I already knew him. It was a comfortable and casual conversation. At the end of it, he grabbed a piece of paper and flipped it over. He scribbled down his cell phone number and told me if I ever needed something or needed help with something to just give him a call.

Was it worth it to play big? I believe so because I now have him on my speed dial and we spent a significant amount of time with their producers discussing potential story opportunities that we had with our clients. I still have the executive producer's personal contact information in my rolodex as well.

Now when I stand in front of women's groups I tell this story. I use myself as an example that each of us needs to stretch beyond our comfort zone and then when it starts to hurt, stretch a bit further. Only then will you be able to accomplish more than you have ever dreamed possible.

There have been many other times when I have played big but this one sticks in my mind because of what Rachel said to me. I had instilled in her my beliefs in less than three days on the job. I stand for stretching, learning and growing so why wouldn't I practice what I preach.

Success Tip: What do you stand for? Are you willing to stretch until it hurts? Then are you willing to stretch even further until the pain is almost unbearable? Athletes say there is no gain without pain. I believe this is true in business as well. Learn to play big and tolerate the pain. If you do you will achieve many successes and feel great about yourself.

11

ASK FOR HELP – SEEK AND APPRECIATE SUPPORT

"On your journey to your new goal, you don't have to make the trip alone."
— *Rhonda Abrams, business advisor*

ginger rogers

Ginger Rogers was very close to her mother. This is the person that she counted on most in her life for support, guidance and direction. She turned to her mother from the beginning of her career through to the last days. Ginger understood the need for support in order to allow herself to flourish and grow.

I believe the most successful people in this world are those that recognize the areas where they need support. Ginger understood that and it was her mother that she turned to time and time again. Her mother understood the Hollywood games and the political nuances that make the entertainment world tick.

Every time Ginger had an issue with the studios, her manager or on set, she turned to her mother for advice, assistance and support. She so often fought the uphill battle and tried to do it with grace and dignity, but that wasn't always easy. It took the support of her mother to help her climb her way to the top and become as successful as she was. Her mother was instrumental in contract negotiations and helping Ginger stand up for herself. One quality that women even today struggle with.

I cannot imagine what different twists and turns Ginger's career would have taken had she not asked for the support from her mother. Without that safety net, I believe that Ginger would have really struggled with her head trash and may not have completed the contract negotiations and achievements that she did.

Sheila Johnson

Many people don't take the time to look past the facts of Sheila Johnson to understand what she accomplished. Many only view her as the first African American billionaire, having been designated that before Oprah Winfrey, and the co-founder of Black Entertainment Television. Yet her background shows more of who she really is.

Sheila Crump Johnson was born in a suburb of Chicago and her father was a neurosurgeon. Throughout all of her school years, she yearned to become a concert violinist. She would often sneak down to the kitchen late at night to practice her violin. After graduating high school, Sheila headed off to the University of Illinois where she rose to the rank of concertmaster in the Illinois All-State Orchestra.

It was while she was at the University of Illinois that she met Robert Johnson. They were married and after she graduated in 1970, they moved to Washington, D.C. It was there that Robert starting dabbling into the cable industry. Sheila found herself supporting him unwaveringly in his efforts. She is quoted as saying that she always put him first. She knew who he was and knew who she was. She was his best friend, his greatest supporter and believed in him before he believed in himself.

For years, Sheila assumed this role yet she was dissatisfied with this role. She detested living up under the cloud of "Wife of." She could not stand going places where the focus was solely on the men and the wives were sitting around like they didn't exist. She would be introduced as "The wife of…" She also felt alienated and did not approve of the raunchy direction that the programming of BET took in the 1990's. Sheila was fired in 1999 by her husband and then they were divorced in 2002.

Sheila's spunky approach to her role in co-founding BET and helping her husband build the company to a multi-billion dollar level could be attributed to her closest supporters. Her mother and her mentor, Susan Sterrett. Sheila's mother taught her not to accept mediocrity, to be the best and never give up. Susan was her orchestra director and she set the standard for how to grow gracefully and deal with people. She taught Sheila to accept people for who they are and it was her inner strength and moral stability that Sheila really admires. Sheila tries hard to emulate her and set her own standards by hers. For Sheila, Susan is the one person in life that she knows she can trust with any information.

Sheila believes that as women are growing up, they really need to find out who they are and what they're about. They need to learn not to let anyone else make those decisions for them. Young women often find themselves defined by the male in their lives. They need to find their own strengths and understand their weaknesses and build a solid character base that is moral and ethical. Too often she believes that women look outside for definition and they sell themselves short.[xxiv]

Sheila holds the "first woman to have" title in many categories. She is now remarried and continues to be an admirable role model for women throughout the world. It is her spirit and desire for surrounding herself with the support she needs that I believe makes her great. You can take a person with a great heart, but without the ability to ask for help and seek support, the impact is limited. I admire her courage to speak up and share her voice and passion for helping women, from the inside out.

my story

It is difficult for women to ask for help. We are very talented and accustomed to giving of our time, our resources and our energy. Yet when it comes time to ask for help, we are often at a loss. Many believe that asking for help is a sign of weakness, admitting of defeat, admitting of ignorance, and so on and so on. That is not the case.

We have no problem stopping and asking for directions if we are lost so why should we have a difficult time asking for help with our business? I learned years ago to ask for help and it has made a tremendous difference for me. I realized that I didn't know all that I needed to know. I wish I would have realized this when I started my advertising agency. Once I discovered this, I decided to ask for help.

Clark Trammell was the executive with an organization that became my first client. My so-called agency which consisted of me, my mother and a few contractors pulled off a tremendous feat. We flawlessly orchestrated an international event complete with media pool feeds, crisis control and on-site production. It was not easy but we rallied the troops we needed, succeeded and made money.

We only had about six months to complete the entire project. In that time I got to know Clark and his team very well. When we were done with the project Clark moved on to turnaround Coach USA and we stayed in constant contact. Over the next couple of years he became my mentor and I have cherished this relationship ever since.

When I started to ask questions, he gladly gave me answers. Answers that were based upon his 30+ years of business experience and answers that he believed would help me get through the crisis I was in or the situation I was faced with. In the beginning it was hard for me to ask that first question. But once I got past that, I realized that a mentor is an invaluable part of your business team.

He has been instrumental to me. He has coached me through the tough times when I didn't know how I was going to make payroll to the exciting times when I was about to meet a celebrity and uncertain of how to act and what to say to negotiating my large contract. Calm and collected describes his approach. He has taught me to be more patient and that in business it's about the long-term play. Not all great success will come in a short amount of time. It often takes years to build and requires layers upon layers of experience and relationships.

Success Tip: Do you have a mentor in your life? Have you asked for help yet? Are you willing to ask for help or are you too caught up in the negative head-trash? Once you get past that, find a mentor and start asking, you will receive and you will reap the rewards more than ten fold. That's my first hand experience.

12

What you Visualize you Materialize

"Have the courage to write down your dream for yourself."
— *May Sarton, poet*

ginger rogers

Ginger Rogers watched her mother, Lela, carefully as she set an example of what you visualize you materialize. Lela knew what she wanted and saw what would be taking shape for Ginger as well. She was right about ninety eight percent of the time. Ginger referred to this ability as her mother's foresight. When in reality, today we know that she was merely visualizing what she was materializing for herself and for Ginger.

When Ginger was starting out in vaudeville, her mother was on the phone with friends exclaiming that Ginger was just getting started. Her mother started touting that Ginger would be in movies next. This embarrassed Ginger at the time, but her mother was right.

Ginger was too naïve at the time and did not possess the business acumen to distinguish the good guys in business from the bad guys. So she relied heavily on her mother to not only visualize the next steps, but to also help guide Ginger in taking those next steps. Each step lead to what her mother had visualized for Ginger. And yes, she was in movies not too long after her mother had been touting that to all of her friends. Ginger followed her mother's instincts all throughout her career. Her mother was almost always by her side and if she wasn't physically there, Ginger was on the phone with her consulting about the next film picture and deal that she was doing.

Ginger saw early on that her mother visualized her success well before Ginger could ever even imagine what her career would morph into. That made her tie with her mother even stronger and she trusted her implicitly with her business decisions. Her mother was right and was able to visualize Ginger's moves that did actually materialize.[xxv]

celine dion

Celine was the youngest of thirteen brothers and sisters. She always considered herself an accidental child and believed that her mother would have rather had more time to do her own things than raise another child. But because her twin brothers were heading off to school, it meant that when Celine was born, she was the primary focus of her mother's attention.

She was treated like an adult from an early age. Her parents explained things to her and eliminated the curiosity that exists so many times in children. She was a well-behaved child early on and loved to sing. It was no wonder. Singing was in her family and Celine was no exception.

She started singing at an early age and performed for the first time when she was five years old. Her mother had a vision for her. She knew at an early age that Celine was destined for greatness and would be a professional singing star. She had that vision and then shared that vision with Celine. At the age of twelve, Celine believed that singing was her future. That became her sole focus and consumed her life.

Her mother told her that in order to get ahead, she would need to be chosen by a great agent and that she would need her own songs. She did not want Celine imitating others. She needed to be able to own her own songs and create her own sound. Celine was committed to finding her own sound. She practiced day in and day out. Singing all of the greats and at first, she imitated each singer. Then she started to slowly bring in sounds and use techniques unique only to this little twelve year old Celine.

Celine sang "Let's get Physical" at a party on a golf course and a man was there that handled several large rock groups in Quebec, Canada. He told Celine that she was good. Very good in fact. That was music to her ears and boosted her confidence level even higher because up to that point she only had praises from her family. This was an "outsider" that worked with professional performers for a living. This meant a lot to Celine. He also went on to tell her that she would need a demo and would need her own songs featured on that demo because of her age and to showcase her unique talent.

She didn't have any songs of her own. But her mother set out that night to write one for her. As Celine went to bed her mother went to work on a song. She had part of it completed by the next morning and called her son Jacques to the house to help her. After numerous attempts and hours of toiling over it, Celine piped up and said, "It doesn't work. That's not it." Having heard that enough, her mother turned to her and said if she was that smart then she should be able to figure it out.

Celine did. She had to hum it first, then the words came and then she put it all together. She had put the finishing touches on her first song. One that was specifically written for her and her own voice. They went to the studio and produced this song along with two others. The demo sounded great and everyone in the family was pleased. Celine recalled one of her family members suggesting sending the demo to René Angélil who at that time was one of the most important record producers in Quebec.

Celine's mother carefully prepared the package. She wrapped it in brown paper with a neatly tied red ribbon, almost like a gift. Celine's brother Paul was in charge of delivering the package and her mother told Celine to keep her fingers crossed and to keep singing.

The family heard nothing. No response from the demo they had sent. Everyone was surprised knowing that producers are always looking for new talent. They kept asking why he or someone from his office didn't at least reply. Even if he wasn't interested, at least give them the courtesy of letting them know.

Celine's brother Michel was a strong-willed person and he knew that once René (now Celine's husband) heard Celine sing, he would be impressed. Michel called and called Rene's office. He kept calling until he finally got him on the phone. He said, "I know you haven't listened to the demo of my sister. 'Cause if you had, you would have already called us." René said that he would probably be listening to demos in the next few days and then he asked how old Michel's sister was. He hesitated and then told René she was twelve. René clearly told Michel that this niche was already taken in the Canadian market. Michel insisted that René listen to the demo and that he would clearly see that Celine marks her own territory and was not like any other singer, young or old.

Just after he insisted René listen, he hung up the phone. Michael turned to the family and told them with great confidence that René would be calling back in ten minutes. He knew it and had visualized it. He was right. The phone rang and it was René. Michel laughed and then told him that Celine could sing anywhere at any time. He hung up the phone and was smiling brightly as he told Celine to get ready, she would be singing for René at two o'clock.

No one knew it at the time, but that phone call changed Celine's life, her family's and would also change René's. When Celine's mother revealed the career that she had mapped out for Celine, there was no doubt. It was logical, possible, sure and certain. Celine never doubted that things would happen like they did. She also never doubted that things would be good, in fact she believed they would be better than good. She was certain that she had everything she needed to succeed. She visualized herself and never doubted. She put herself out there and played full out without doubt.[xxvi]

We all know that today she is married to René and they have a beautiful son. She is extremely wealthy in many aspects of her life. It is a testament to the fact that what you visualize you can materialize. Remove all doubt, have no fear and play full out. That's how you achieve all that you can achieve and be all that you can be.

my story

I remember reading the Secret for the first time several years ago. As I read it I realized that some things I had been doing subconsciously in my life was impacting me both positively and negatively. The first time I read the book I was in many ways doubtful of the words I was reading. I found myself questioning instead of embracing. It wasn't until the third or fourth time of reading the book that I started to apply each principle to every aspect of my life. I was then able to recite instances where the book's principles were upheld in my own life.

Then I started to examine the areas where I did not have more than I wanted. Areas where I knew I wanted to increase the level of abundance became my focus. I delved deep within myself to understand why I was not achieving what I wanted in every aspect of my life.

What I found is that I had not fully visualized myself in the situation where I wanted to be. I had started to but had let fear and doubt cloud the picture. These feelings masked the true inner feeling and prevented all of my senses from experiencing what I was visualizing.

Through journaling, I was able to understand my fears and then eliminate them one by one. Once I had accomplished that, then I was free to fully experience what I was visualizing. I had removed the cloud of doubt and could let the sun shine freely on my desires, wants and needs.

It was at that moment that I started to experience the true meaning of what you visualize you materialize. I started to manifest people in my life, resources and relationships that were all part of taking me to the next level both personally and professionally. I stopped doubting my abilities and stopped putting up the road blocks that as women, we are so good at. Bottom line, I dumped my head-trash and was free of the clutter so that I could thoroughly enjoy and reap the rewards of my efforts.

I will not say this is an easy process. People often ask me how I have been able to meet the people I have in such a short amount of time. I tell them that it has taken me years to get to the point where I am truly balanced and at peace with myself. I understand my true purpose and mission on this earth. I know without a doubt why I was put here and have painted the picture of the impact that I want to have on others.

That was hard work getting to this point. But now that I am in this space, I am able to manifest things often in less than a day. There are occasions where it will take me longer, but my point is that when the energy and focus have no clouds and restraints, then you are free to be, do and experience.

How do you know what you want to visualize? How do you create a reminder that helps keep you focused? In the Secret the authors talk about a vision board. I have a vision board not because it reminds me of the material things that I want to purchase. Rather I know that when I have the money to purchase a car that I have identified then I will have the resources needed to start the Women's Empowerment Center foundation. I have spoken with many people, women especially, that are not always comfortable identifying "things" for their vision board. I believe that true wealth is when all of your accounts are full, including happiness, health, relationships, spirituality, and money. My recommendation is to identify the things you want to purchase and also incorporate things that will evoke a feeling inside of you. What represents happiness for you? What represents healthy living? What represents true spirituality? Find images that your mind can start associating with these feelings and you will be able to truly materialize what you visualize.

One thing that is not always highlighted in all of the self-help programs is that it is hard and it takes a lot of work. When you start to visualize don't expect to instantly materialize the things you want. It takes work and often times it is hard along the way. But everything in this world that is worth doing is not always easy.

Remembering this is key when we live in a society that is all about instant gratification. We want a single pill to lose weight, we want a drink for unlimited energy, we want instant gratification in nearly every aspect of our lives and that is what our society is breeding. Remember that this process is different and it will require work, you will need to take action, you will need to become100% committed, you will need to be willing to endure the pain that may be associated with such growth and you will need to be prepared that the journey will be hard.

Once you get your mind in such a state of focus that you are physically and mentally able to overcome all obstacles to achieve what you visualize, then you are poised to manifest at a level few can. This is viewed by many as utopia because you set yourself apart and let the negative words of others float off of you like water on a duck's back. Nothing phases you in this state and you put yourself in a position of sheer determination, focus and power that tells the universe that you are a force to be reckoned with. Few people will want to challenge you because the energy they will need to expend is tremendous. At this level people will feel your energy and will quickly understand the magnitude of what you are doing.

This entire concept of what you visualize you materialize can be overwhelming to many people. I suggest that you start and take things one step at a time. Focus on identifying your passion. Then when you have that figured out, take one aspect of your life that you want to improve. Visualize what it would look like the way you ultimately want it. Then remove all of the fear and doubt around this new image. Allow all of your senses to experience the new vision. Then create a vision board that will serve as a daily reminder of these feelings. Ensure that you have locked in the feelings with the images. You can accomplish this by getting the senses truly in tune, feeling the feelings from head to toe, then identify these feelings with the images that you are viewing. Anchor them in strongly and know that it will likely take several exercises to truly anchor these feelings. Then stay focused. Put the energy out into the universe and never let anyone steer you wrong.

Just as Celine Dion knew that she was destined to be a great performer. She saw herself on stage with crowds of people and this was all at the tender age of twelve.

Success Tip: No matter what your age, you too can experience this same level of satisfaction. You can become a master at manifesting and will increase all of the wealth accounts in your life. The tip is ignoring the head-trash that you have and honoring where you are today.

13

Watch the Road Signs and the Road will Pave Itself in Front of You

"If you keep following your own footprints, you will end up where you began, but if you stretch yourself you will flourish."

— *Donna Baspaly, artist*

ginger rogers

The first time Ginger met Fred Astaire it was all but glamorous. He had been brought in by one of the movie producers to polish up a few dance moves. Fred was able to tighten some of the unpolished moves the choreographer had in place. Ginger danced with Fred and quickly fell into step. He was easy to follow and they glided across the floor like they had been dancing together for years.

Ginger had no real reason to be impressed with him and never thought of him again. This was a road sign, yet Ginger didn't see it or pay attention to it.

Some time had passed and the phone rang in Ginger's apartment. Her mother answered and then told Ginger that the man said he was Fred Astaire. Ginger thought it was one of her friends playing a prank on her so she answered the phone with a funny voice.

Low and behold, it was Fred. She quickly gained her composure and apologized for her change in voice. Fred told her that he had been meaning to call her for some time. He wanted to take her out to dinner. She quickly accepted and then acted like a young school girl for just a short while. Then she regained her composure. After all, he wasn't that great of a dancer and Ginger remembered having danced with several other men that she could glide across the floor with. She convinced herself that she didn't need to put on a fuss or get all giddy. Then Thursday night arrived and she did get nervous and giddy. Ginger fussed over what to wear, her hair and the many little details to get ready for her date.

He picked her up at the theater at midnight. They went to the Casino in the Park which was a magical place. There was a dreamy atmosphere there with unforgettable aromas that danced on their noses. As soon as they ordered their food, Fred asked Ginger to dance. She gracefully accepted and was then pleasantly surprised. He led her around the dance floor with such ease and grace. He was also quite the conversationalist which impressed Ginger. Most of the men she had danced with could not talk and dance at the same time.

Even the band leader commented on how lovely they looked dancing together on the floor. They seemed to glide gently as one. They completed the last dance and Fred's chauffer drove them through the park to Ginger's building. Fred hugged her and they had a nice kiss, according to Ginger anyway.

This was 1930 and it wasn't until 1933 that they starred in their first movie together. The road signs were there three years prior to the first film. Everyone around them saw the road signs, yet they both believed it was just nice dance moves that they were doing casually on a date. Little did they know, that would be the start of a long relationship on screen that would fascinate many and mesmerize most.

Road signs are interesting. They are always there, yet it is a matter of who's looking and paying attention.[xxvii]

tina turner

Tina Turner (born Anna Mae Bullock) was born in the south into a family of sharecroppers. At the age of ten, Anna and her sister were abandoned by their mother. Just three years later, their father left them. Deserted and desolate, they were raised by their cousins and grandmother. Shifted from one place to another during their childhood they lived with this arrangement and at the age of sixteen, Tina's grandmother died.

Tina decided to move to St. Louis where she heard her mother was living. Not for sure if her mother would be receptive to her or not, she took a chance and moved. She arrived in St. Louis and was quickly introduced to the world of rhythm and blues. She would regularly frequent the Club Manhattan and started to date the lead saxophonist of one of the popular bands. Then one night, Tina was called on stage to sing. She eagerly jumped up and belted out the song. She caught the eye of the leader of the band, Ike Turner.

Nothing happened immediately. Tina just kept hanging out at the club and with the band members. Then, two years later, she was in a recording studio hanging out with the band when one of the singers didn't show up for the recording session. Ike asked her to step up and fill in knowing full well that he would end up replacing the vocals with the other woman but at least it would keep things moving forward. Tina stepped up and sang her heart out. The song was "A Fool In Love" and when Ike heard her spine tingling performance, he was convinced to keep her vocals and to make her part of the band. He changed her name to Tina Turner and made her a full part of the band just before the song hit the airwaves.

Tina had not planned a career in music. She had merely moved to St. Louis following the road signs that indicated her mother might be there. Yet she was flexible and in the right place at the right time. That set her career in motion and gave her a lifetime of entertainment. Ike and Tina were a resounding success. Today we know that after suffering years of abuse, she finally left Ike with only thirty-six cents in her pocket and a petrol card.

I believe something triggered in her. Something caused her to wake up and watch the new road signs. Since then her road has been paved with great success.

my story

I spent the majority of my life being inflexible. Moving one calculated step at a time to achieve the goals that I had put forth for myself. Knowing that each step would build upon the other taking me that much closer to my ultimate goals. For years my mentor, Clark, has told me that if you just watch the road signs, the road will pave itself in front of you. I listened to him, but I never believed him. I was always taught that you have to take the steps that you have laid for yourself and follow the plan. Create the plan and work the plan and work the plan and work the plan.

How could reading the road signs work? What were the road signs? I remember hearing him say this for years but it wasn't until I survived my COD that I sat and thought about what he had been saying. I pondered what it would be like to have a plan that was merely a guiding light that would lead me to my future, not a hard and fast road that had to be followed one step at a time.

It was difficult for me, but I started to try and expand my mind. I viewed the business plans and my life goals as a beacon of light that were merely guiding me in the right direction. Then I allowed myself to read the road signs and make turns, twists and climb hills along the way. All knowing that I was and still am moving toward the beacon of light. I have spent the last four years living my life and guiding my business with this philosophy.

What an exciting journey it has been. I never realized how many opportunities I passed up or that blew by me because I was too focused to see them. Many of us tend to go full pedal to the metal only glancing at the dashboard and watching the road straight ahead of us. Then when we have to hit the brakes because the bridge is out, the only question we ask is, "Why didn't someone tell me the bridge was out?" In fact, there were numerous signs warning that there was danger ahead and that a detour or different course would need to be taken, however being so focused on the road in front of you and with the pedal to the metal, all of these signs were ignored.

What are road signs? As I opened my life and my mind to knew experiences and ways of viewing things, I began to quiz my mentor on a regular basis. I asked him to identify the road signs that he watches and then I asked how he reads and interprets them. I felt like I was six years old again and one question led to another which led immediately to another.

Thank heavens Clark is a patient man. He answered every question for me and often answered with another question to make me think and to challenge my current views. What I found out is that we are surrounded with road signs every day. They can be your horoscope, cancelled planes, missed phone calls, missed appointments, introductions, meetings with intuitive people and seemingly coincidental occurrences yet they are all road signs.

Clark told me that by combining and reading all of the road signs, you have a clearer picture as to what your next move needs to be. Often several signs come together to tell you to turn one direction or another or to stop for a breather. I believe each woman needs to have her own secret set of basic road signs to read and then maintain an open mind to the other influences in life.

Let me give you an example of how reading the road signs and being flexible can make your life easier, more enjoyable and more productive. It was the day before Thanksgiving and we were trying to get things wrapped up for a four day holiday weekend. We had our production schedule in order and had things planned down to the minute for the following week. The phone rang and it was Les Brown asking if I could meet him in Phoenix on Sunday of the holiday weekend. He told me that he would be there filming his PBS special and he wanted me to meet the producers and people there.

I told him to give me an hour and I would move my schedule around so that I could be there. I had not planned to be traveling the following week. I had not planned the expense. We had just mapped out all of the work and confirmed appointments for the following week and our schedule was already tight. We had client meetings and conference calls on the books.

I knew that this was a road sign. So, we jumped into action and started rearranging the entire schedule. Bought the plane ticket and I worked part of the weekend in order to have things caught up. We had the plan. I would fly Monday morning and take an early morning flight home Tuesday to be in Denver for my 10 am meeting. I arrived at the airport first thing Monday morning and my flight was cancelled. This was a major travel day since it was right after Thanksgiving weekend.

I remembered the road signs. I didn't get upset. Although there was a plane full of people that were all very upset, angry, cursing and raising cane with the agents. Now that I have shifted my mind set, I don't get upset anymore. I went to another agent and found out that all of the flights were booked the entire day so I started working with the agent to see if my mileage status would help and to determine if there were any other options. While she was checking, I called the office and decided that if I wasn't going to get into Phoenix until late in the day, I would just cancel all of my Denver meetings Tuesday and fly home Tuesday night instead of first thing in the morning.

All the changes were made through the office and I arrived in Phoenix late afternoon. I got there and called my friend with Dr. John Gray's office and told her that I would now be in town Tuesday. Asked if she had time for lunch so that we could catch up. Low and behold, she not only invited me to lunch but to meet Brian Tracy. She couldn't believe the coincidence as he was only going to be in town on Tuesday.

Here is a recap of the trip and the opportunities that were presented to me because the road signs were clear, my flight was cancelled:

1) Met a famous entertainer – She was meeting with Les in the hotel but because I was late, he moved his meetings around and I was there for the meeting and had an extensive conversation with her. Turns out she is in need of marketing strategy and I have a contact with a national entertainment venue which is what she is looking for in her new venture.

2) Met the producer of the television special in Phoenix as well as one from Chicago and an executive producer who was visiting about another opportunity to create a weekly television program geared toward women. He had been working with a famous woman for over a year but it was just not working out and he had just made the decision to move on and look for someone else. I was in the car as we visited about this possibility.

3) I was supposed to stay with my dear friend at her home but when I sent her a text message at 10 pm letting her know that I would be late getting finished with the taping and that I could just get a hotel if I needed to. Her response was simple. She was sick with a terrible cold and indicated that I would not want to be around her anyway.

4) We left the taping and headed back to the hotel where Les and I were able to meet one on one for the next two hours.

5) Tuesday I met Brian Tracy and get a video segment shot with him discussing the value of ilearningglobal for entrepreneurs around the country. I then was able to meet the entire board of directors for the company and have lunch with my dear friend Sherrie that works with Dr. John Gray.

All of this because my flight was cancelled and my friend got sick. If I had been on my original flight, I would not have stayed an extra day and would not have been able to meet Brian Tracy. I would have stayed with my friend and would not have had the one on one time with Les to map out some significant business opportunities.

Road signs are around you everyday. When there is resistance or what seems to be a challenge in front of you, step back and open your eyes. Recognize that there are road signs all around you, you just need to take notice of them, read them and then move forward.

I understand that this may sound like a foreign concept, it was for me at first as well. I liked things to go according to plan and I liked to have the structure in place. Understand, I still have basic structure in place, I am just flexible enough to allow other opportunities to enter into my life and pave a new path to that beacon of light I am moving toward.

Women often have a difficult time applying this in business. It is often viewed as an easier concept to grasp personally. Yet professionally women so often believe you have to hold hard and fast to the business plans. Let me give you an example of how reading the road signs work in biz.

I had spent nearly two months working with our advertising agency on new packaging designs for our product. As we looked at sketches and renderings, I kept asking about the per unit cost to ensure that it would be aligned with the budget and would be produced in a timely fashion. Each time I asked, I was assured that was the case and I was told not to worry.

So I didn't. Two weeks later, I received the dreaded phone call. The creative director informed me that the pricing had come back for the packaging and it was twice the budget and would take a third longer than what we specified. He was mortified and extremely disappointed because we had wasted nearly two months working with this firm and we did not have another two months to start over with a new company. He was extremely upset and I merely reassured him that this was a road sign. I wasn't sure what the next step would be but that I was confident things were unfolding for a reason. I told him to sit tight and within a week or so I felt things would iron out and we would have a direction to move. He was shocked that I was not upset. Why should I be upset? It wasn't his fault and I knew it was a sign, I just didn't know what direction we would be going.

The following week I hopped on a plane to San Diego for an important meeting with an international strategic alliance partner. We were sitting in the Four Season's meeting room when we started discussing a retail distribution channel idea. Within one hour a major international retailer was on the phone and there was interest. I stepped out of the meeting and called the Creative Director. I told Eric that the resistance we got on the packaging was a road sign. We didn't need that design because it would not allow us to enter the retail market. We needed a design that was more compact and had a cost 80% less than what we had specified.

By the time I arrived back in Denver the next day, the agency had a new packaging design concept prepared and had located a Denver based software packaging company that could produce the design for just over three dollars as compared to sixty dollars with the other company and other design. Plus, this design was one third of the size of the other packaging which would give us ultimate flexibility with shelf space.

Road signs...they are powerful and if you calmly stay focused on moving toward the beacon of light and read the road signs, you will not be lead astray. Years ago I would have handled these situations much differently. I would have been extremely upset that my flight was cancelled. I would have likely fired the advertising agency or someone for wasting two months in packaging design that didn't work. Yet, I learned from Clark that all of the road signs lead us down a better path if we are just flexible enough to read them and more importantly follow the new path.

Are you flexible enough to read the road signs around yourself and follow them in your personal life as well as with your business? That is the real question because once you get your mindset shifted and your energy is focused on being flexible and adaptable then your senses will become more keenly attuned with the road signs that are around you every day.

These are just two minor examples of how road signs have lead me closer to the beacon of light that is guiding my business and my life. Take time to step back and look at things around you. Look at resistance as merely the warning sign that something better is about to be revealed. Be flexible to go with the flow as they say.

Have you ever watched a willow flow in the wind? It sways one direction and then freely moves in another direction. The point is that the willow branch flows. You need to flow in your life as well. Be flexible and aware of the road signs that are around you each and every day. These are what will shape the ultimate success and greatness you will achieve.

Success Tip: What if there are drastic and horrible things happening? I know it is hard to believe, but they are road signs as well. Something better will come about if you are flexible and have the faith to keep moving.

14

TRUST YOUR INTUITION - IT CAN BE YOUR BEST GUIDE

"If you want easy, don't become an entrepreneur."
— *Carol Columbus Green, CEO Laracris*

ginger rogers

It was April and Ginger was about to celebrate her first birthday. Her mother had gotten busy in a mountain of paperwork at the Sand Company and had neglected to look out the window and check in on Ginger. It had been a bit of time and when she realized that she had gotten lost, Lela jumped up and looked out the window. She didn't see Ginger anywhere.

She ran outside and still could not find the little girl. At first she thought that Ginger had just gone on a little bit of an adventure so she waited about fifteen minutes. When Ginger was nowhere to be found, Lela started to panic. The Sand Company was next to the railroad tracks and they were filled with Pullman cars. Lela ran over and flew up and down the steps of the Pullman car. Asking every person she saw and no one had seen Ginger. Someone suggested to her that perhaps someone had taken her little girl.

Lela left the station and went to the police and filed the necessary reports. The headline in the newspaper the next day read: "Virginia McMath Kidnapped." Lela made her way to her parents house where she prayed and cried. With one knock on the door, new light was shed on her the kidnapping. A man appeared and stated that he saw a little girl sitting in the lap of a man on the train to St. Louis and the girl would not stop crying. Then it hit Lela. Her former husband had kidnapped the little girl. As she started out the door to catch a train to St. Louis, she remembered that there was once discussion about moving to Texas. She racked her brain to remember the name of the town where his cousin lived.

She knew in her gut that he had taken Ginger and that he was headed to Texas. It wasn't a description or any other factual information. It was Lela's gut instinct that led her in this direction. When she arrived at the train station, she purchased a ticket to Ennis, Texas. She was antsy on the train and when it arrived, she found a cab and gave him the address of Eddins' (her former husband) cousin.

They arrived at the home and she politely asked the driver to wait. She approached the front door and as she looked through the screen, she saw Ginger sitting in a high chair. She flung the door open, ran in and grabbed her little girl. She ran out the door and hopped in the cab shouting, "Go, go!" The women of the house were not far behind her but the taxis sped off before the ladies could reach the car door.

The taxi pulled into the train station just as the last train was departing. Lela was frantic. What would she do? Where would she go? The cab driver sensed her panic and offered to drive her to his mother's teepee where she could safely stay the night. Then he explained that he would gladly drive her in the morning to the station to catch the first train. Lela held off her fear that Eddins would come looking for her on the first morning train. She just couldn't think of it at that time. She had to remain calm.

Lela was right. When she arrived at the station in the morning to purchase her train tickets, the station master said there was a man that was waiting in the storm cellar. Lela sent the taxi driver to see if it indeed was Eddins. When he came back, he told her it was in fact him. Then he reassured her that she had no need to worry because he had barricaded the storm cellar door and it would take him up to three hours to break out. By that time, Lela and the baby would be safely on their way.

They indeed did board the train and made their way safely home. Lela Did trust her intuition and it was right. If she hadn't, it is hard to tell what would have happened to poor little Ginger. Things would have certainly been different. Lela is like many women that find it easier to trust their intuition in their personal lives yet have a more difficult time trusting it in business.

฿ara blakely

Working as a sales trainer by day and performing stand-up comedy at night, Sara Blakely didn't know the first thing about the pantyhose industry (except she dreaded wearing pantyhose). She came up with a new concept. She cut the bottoms out of her pantyhose and started to try her new concept. She had never taken a business class which made the process even more challenging. As a result, she only had one place to operate from and that was her gut. She new in her gut that other women felt the same as she did about pantyhose: that the purpose was to cover the gut without being uncomfortable.

She had read several books on trademarks and patents and spent countless hours in the library researching. Through her research, she realized that there wasn't a product like hers that was patented. She approached several lawyers who thought she was crazy and even a few thought she had been sent by Candid Camera, the prankster T.V. program

She decided to write the patent herself to keep costs to a minimum and then she finally found a lawyer that wrote the claims for her.

The next step was like a mountain in front of her. How was she going to get the product manufactured? She approached several manufacturers and she took a week off of work to drive all around North Carolina meeting with them. Actually begging them to make her idea a reality. They always asked her the same three questions. 1) And you are? 2) And you are representing? 3) And you are financially backed by? She would simply answer Sara Blakely to all three questions and if that wasn't enough to send her packing, the minute she explained the product they truly thought she was crazy. They said it made no sense and would not sell. Then, two weeks later, Sara received a call from an owner of one of the manufacturing facilities. He said that he decided to help make her crazy idea a reality.

When Sara asked why he changed his mind. Turns out he had two daughters that didn't think the idea was so crazy. It took her one year to perfect the prototype because Sara was obsessed with comfort and she wanted to make sure it could be worn everyday so she wore it everyday.

She could have cut corners, saved time and completed the prototype sooner but she was committed to quality and comfort. She knew that the time she spent testing and wearing the product would be well worth it when she took the product to market.

Now that she had a product, she needed a name. She knew from her standup comedy days that the letter K is known to make people laugh. All of a sudden she was hit by the word Spanks. Then she did some research and determined that made up words are easier to trademark so she changed the K to an X. The name makes people laugh, makes their mind wander and it is designed to make women's butts and guts look better so why not?

Sara spent hours in the stores looking at pantyhose packaging. And her comment was the same for all of them. Boring. She believed it was time for a bold new change. She created the illustrated women on the front of the package and then for the fine print, she purchased ten packages of pantyhose and copied the key information that appeared on all of them. She figured if it was consistently found on all ten packages then it must be important, must be printed for a reason and likely someone spent a significant amount of legal fees to get the words just right.

Then at the last minute after consulting with her mom to test the offensive factor, they added the tagline, "Don't worry, we've got your butt covered." They all laughed hysterically.

Now, with packaging completed, Sara had to really be creative to get the product out to market. She didn't have a marketing budget. Heck, she didn't even have any money. She got a break when she called the buyer for Nieman Marcus and said that she had the ultimate product for her shoppers and if she would give her just ten minutes she would fly to Dallas. The buyer agreed. Sara hopped a plane with her prototype product in her lucky backpack. She promptly took the buyer to the ladies room and showed her the before and after in her most appropriate cream pants.

That was it, the buyer loved the product and it was put on the shelves. Sara enlisted friends and family to help rally and get buzz around the product. Since she didn't have a promotions budget, let alone a budget at all, she traveled the country for the first year showing associates the product and then staying for the day to do in store demonstrations.

The momentum built and she landed herself on Oprah, the Today Show, The Big Idea and numerous other television programs. She was also featured in several magazines.

Sara trusted her gut yet again when she left Spanx for a three month stint on the reality television show with Sir Richard Branson. People told her that she was crazy. She didn't know what it was, but her gut told her that it was a chance of a lifetime. She followed her gut and as they traveled around the world, Sara was able to visit with Sir Richard Branson and pick his brain on his global foundation, Virgin Unite. She wanted to know how he set it up and how it worked. Sara had a dream of starting a foundation and this was an opportunity to learn from one of the greats.

In an unexpected twist at the conclusion of the program, Branson handed Sara a check for $750,000. That was his paycheck from Fox television for the show. Turns out Sir Richard Branson felt strongly about Sara's passion to start her own foundation. Shocked, amazed, and excited, Sara set out to get the details in place.

He then joined her in Atlanta in 2006 to launch the Sara Blakely Foundation, which is dedicated to helping women globally through education and entrepreneurship.

Trust your gut. There is a funny thing in this world called intuition and for some reason, women are blessed with it yet we are told to stifle it. Women are told that following or listening to our gut isn't a good way to do business. Lead with your head first then your gut.[xxviii]

Wrong. Sara trusted her gut and look at the breaks and successes that she experienced because of it.

my story

Have you ever had a bad gut feeling about a business deal yet ignored it and went ahead only to find out your gut was right? I have on numerous occasions and now trust my gut implicitly. I look inward for confirmation in my gut first, then I explore the financial aspects of the business deal.

It was the "myagencydot com" era and start-up's were a dime a dozen. I had been referred into a company that needed a brand strategy, marketing and public relations plan as well as all of the implementation tools. They needed brochures, business cards, a Web site, basically all the marketing materials that would be required to support the sales effort and get the company off the ground floor.

I remember meeting with the Executive Vice President, Larry. He was an arrogant man that had supposedly made it big with several other Internet companies. He thought very highly of himself to say the least. In meeting with him my team asked all of the usual questions. And as was befitting of a man like this, he gave cocky and arrogant answers to each question. He often acted disgusted that we even needed to ask the question. He portrayed an attitude that we were beneath him. He's clearly felt he was the expert.

I don't have a problem with that when someone clearly is an expert. Yet every time he opened his mouth it was obvious that he was not the expert he thought he was. We kept up our questioning until we got all of the answers that we needed. As we were wrapping up the meeting he asked for a business card. Then he asked where our office was. I hesitated for a moment because we were officing out of my home and at that time it was not the "right image" whereas today, it is much more common place and acceptable in business to have a home office.

I told him the cross streets thinking this would suffice. Not this man. He kept questioning and probing until I came right out with it and said that my staff and I work remotely. He was disgusted but agreed to review our proposal and recommendations. As we left I remember visiting with Eric about it and we both agreed that Larry could be a difficult man. But we knew with confidence that we had the skills and talents to give them more than they were expecting. We could easily do the job and create a dynamite brand and marketing strategy.

I prepared the proposal and we got the work. As we started through the process, every juncture was a challenge. He was a difficult man that was clearly trying to justify his position. He didn't like anything that we presented. Everything had to be changed. We got to the point where some of his changes took the idea back to our original presentation so it became comical at times.

Then Eric and I presented the logo options. Larry started in and we listened to his thoughts. Always trying to be open to ensure we were delivering what they really needed. Then the President started in. He insisted that Eric, my creative director, pull out his laptop and start making changes to the logo design on the spot. "Try starting with a mountain in the background then add the words in a different text and put this all under a line with, blah, blah, blah, blah," said the President.

It was nerve racking. That's not how we worked. Our process was to discuss the logos then discuss the changes that the client requested. We would then prepare a change order listing all of these out and once signed by our client, we started making the changes. We didn't work on the fly. Creative juices don't work that way. Yet we knew we wanted the business so we felt we were in an awkward position.

We finally convinced the executives that we needed to have time to make the proper changes to the design. Once we got through the logo design we presented business cards and a printing estimate. I emailed the estimate to Larry and remember pulling into the Walmart parking lot one night with my husband. We had a few things to pick up and I just got the car in park when my cell phone rang. It was Larry.

He proceeded to cuss me out. He was yelling so loud that my husband could hear him on the other side of the car. I can tolerate a lot but cursing at me was not one of them. I calmly interrupted him and said, "I will not be spoken to this way. When you can speak professionally and calmly I will take your call. Until then this conversation is done." And I hung up.

I went in the following week and told them that we would be wrapping up the final couple of projects and they would be on their own. We were no longer going to work under those conditions.

I look back on this experience and wonder why I ever took them on as a client. My gut was flashing neon signals from the first meeting. Telling me that they were going to be extremely difficult, hard to please and likely would have a problem with everything presented.

Yet something inside me suppressed my gut and I moved forward. After all, we needed the business. Boy isn't that a famous line that has come back to haunt us all at one point or another.

Over the years I have learned that when my gut is not in check, I listen. I no longer suppress it. In fact I honor it and speak it. People will often hear me say, "I have a good gut feeling about this." Or, "I have a bad feeling. My gut is not in check on this one."

We met with a couple of bankers early 2008 and as we started to talk, one man appeared extremely arrogant. He was demeaning to Rachel and me from the start of the meeting. I kept throwing statistics out, ideas and marketing strategies to get the company launched and where they wanted to be. He didn't want to hear that. He kept talking mumbo jumbo and the final straw for me was when he made a condescending comment and then proceeded to drill it home.

We wrapped up the meeting and I told them to call when they had their ducks in a row. As we got on the elevator, I proclaimed that no amount of money would make me take them on as a client. Life is too short and my gut was completely flashing neon signs.

We didn't work with that client. I have learned that women's intuition is strong, real and applies to business. I don't care what people say, it does apply to business. I have saved myself a lot of agony and frustration by listening to my intuition. It doesn't matter how much money is involved, if you go against your gut it will cost you several times more than the deal is worth.

Success Tip: Do you listen to your intuition in your personal life but not in your professional life? Take time to reflect back on how many times you could have saved yourself agony and pain if you had just listened to your intuition. Start honoring what you have been blessed with as a woman and you will create a better business because of it.

15

SAY NO –
CREATE BALANCE IN YOUR LIFE

"Most of us have trouble juggling. The woman who says that she doesn't is someone whom I admire but have never met."

— *Barbara Walters*

ginger rogers

Ginger Rogers was not exempt from burn out. Her typical schedule was doing eight shows a week, including matinees on Wednesday and Saturday. She was getting up at 6 am to be at the Paramount studios in Long Island where she went through makeup and hairdressing to be on the set at 8 am. Then she would leave there at 6 pm to do Broadway in the evening and sometimes do a gig at a nightclub. Many days she would not get home until 1 a.m.

She had reached that edge in 1937 just after she finished filming Having a Wonderful Time. She was pushed into film retakes, was trying to get wardrobe fittings taken care of for the next film and she had to pose for gallery shots which quickly ate up the five days that she thought she had off.

There was no resting at that point in her life. She was exasperated often as she tried to juggle the daily demands of the studio all the while sacrificing her own personal necessities.

She never seemed to have time for a dressmaker to measure the hems of her dresses or to buy the right shoes for a newly purchased gown, or to have a much-needed manicure or to pluck her eyebrows. She found herself trying to do all of these things herself and on the go. In her career she also had to juggle a voice coach, rehearsals for new routines, photo sessions, interviews and other appointments. They always seemed to get done but not always to her satisfaction.

There were many days when she would work on set filming all day just to leave at the end of most people's day to begin her Broadway performance which lasted until the early hours of the morning. With a few hours of sleep, she was up and back on set for filming again and would repeat the horrendous schedule day in and day out.

Her mother knew the toll this demanding schedule was taking on Ginger. She knew that Ginger was exhausted and exasperated so she decided to plan a getaway for Ginger in Sun Valley. Lela had her new friend make all of the arrangements and it was the perfect trip. Ginger was mentally exhausted and needed time away from the studio.

It also helped give her the stamina she needed to re-negotiate her contract with the studio. Lela knew what the scheduling was doing to Ginger so it made it much easier for her to hold her ground while they renegotiated Ginger's contract.

During that period of time, Ginger realized that she needed to insist on the necessities that would give her the balance that she had to have in life. She was suffering greatly and was just realizing the toll it was taking on her life. Balance is something that women have had a battle with for many years and it still holds true today.[xxix]

gladys knight

Gladys Knight longed for a normal balanced life. From an early age, she was performing on stage in front of audiences. Let's start with a bit of history. Gladys Knight and the Pips were born when she decided to give her brother a surprise birthday party. She had planned everything out to the last detail. They had sandwiches made with chips and what most of us would consider basics but for them was an extravagant treat. Everyone kept saying Gladys would be in trouble because she hadn't asked her mother's permission to spend this amount of money.

But somehow Gladys was prepared to take any heat. She thought it was the appropriate thing to do and she had a lot of fun. When everyone arrived home her brother was surprised and her mother was not angry. She was very pleased that Gladys had gone to so much work to make her brother's birthday so special. They had the neighbor's record player going full blast and everyone was singing and dancing. It was a real party. Until there was a disagreement and the neighbor boy grabbed his record player and went home.

No one was ready to have the evening end so the family hollered for Gladys to sing and encouraged her two cousins to join her. They started to sing and everyone loved it. They were a hit and not just because it was mainly relatives listening. They were truly talented and sounded good together. Even if they hadn't sang together prior to that night.

This set the wheels in motion. They started to tour throughout the country. Small gigs where they would perform in the evening and then drive all night and part of the day to get to the next stop. Sleeping in the car at times and when they had a motel, it was a real treat, a luxury indeed. After high school the pull between her professional and personal life became even greater which made making choices even more difficult than ever before for Gladys.

There was so much that Gladys wanted to do with her singing career yet she dreamed of having some sort of normal structured life outside of show business. In her yearning for both it seemed there was no way to capture both.

Her career continued to take off and the pace and direction were out of her control. Gladys became pregnant and she knew that her mother felt she had fallen into the trap that her mother had seen many other women fall into where they struggle for the rest of their lives. Gladys assured her mother that she would do whatever she had to in order to raise the child properly even if it meant giving up singing and taking on a job waiting tables in a local restaurant.

With high school behind her and Jimmy, her new husband, beside her, they rejoined the band and hit the circuit hard and fast trying to make some money before the baby came. They did as many as sixty-five one night shows in a row with no dressing rooms, bathrooms only when they were lucky and all the smells that you could imagine backstage. But Gladys Knight and the Pips picked up some good moves during that time.

After several months of doing the road houses, they were able to advance to the upper tier of the circuit. They were barely getting by financially, were often hungry and rode crammed for hours at a time in a car. Gladys reached a point where she felt wiped out. The exhaustion hit particularly hard one night as they walked ten blocks to their hotel. It was so bad that she had to keep stopping and sitting along the way. Most of the guys didn't pay much attention to her and Jimmy stayed with her as the rest of the bunch continued on. Jimmy kept encouraging her to keep going, telling her that she could lay down as soon as they got to the hotel. As they continued walking, they reached a sandwich shop. She was certainly hungry and when Jimmy asked if she wanted to stop and get something to eat, she said no.

She didn't feel like stopping. All she wanted to do was crawl in bed. They made it to the hotel and as she crawled in bed, Jimmy headed back to get sandwiches. When he dropped the food off in the hotel room he split to be with the other guys and left Gladys there to rest. She couldn't get comfortable and kept having a pain in her abdomen. She would walk and then lie down, walk and then lie down. Nothing seemed to work and the pain grew so bad that she started to scream and cry. Jimmy was no where to be found so she had to keep talking to herself to try and remain calm. Jimmy finally came back but it was late and she didn't have the energy nor the desire to tell him the pain she was in.

She actually miscarried the baby. She didn't even wake her husband. She decided to deal with it herself and she cried herself back to sleep. She tried to downplay it the following morning and Jimmy wanted her to skip her performance that night. She refused and assured him that she would be alright.

She did what she felt she had to do. She went on stage and performed. She didn't use any ounce of femininity and didn't want sympathy. Yet I can't imagine the pain that she was experiencing deep down and the strength it must have taken to get on the stage that night.

She knew that she had pushed herself too hard for too long. She did not feel balanced and had not taken enough care of herself. That's just how Gladys was though and how hard she went. Like many women, she would put up a front in public. She thought that if she smiled through it and stayed busy that everything would return back to normal. However this was clearly a state of denial.

Gladys suffered many triumphs and many difficult situations. She always yearned for balance and a sense of normalcy. Even though she admits that most of her life was out of balance it was in her mid-forties that she felt she finally gained the balance in her life that she had been searching for. She decided she wanted to do it all again on her own. She launched her own career in Las Vegas without the Pips. She followed this with an HBO television special and a short-lived sitcom.

In 1996 she performed at Madison Square Garden which brought back memories for her performance when she was eight. That's when she won the Ted Mack championship. Just as when she was eight, she finished and was greeted with a standing ovation that brought her to tears. It was at that moment she realized how far she had come, how much she had survived and how well her gift had served her throughout her life.[xxx]

my story

My story is based upon the real life value of achieving and maintaining balance in your life. Too often we are so focused on running our business that we get off kilter. I already explained to you how I drove myself to reach my Crap Out Date.

After I started working with Dr. John Gray who authored Men are from Mars, Women are from Venus, I realized that there were natural chemical reasons why I was feeling a certain way. First of all, I have weighed nearly 40 pounds more than I do now. I went from a size 14 to a size 6. When I gained the weight, I was extremely stressed. I would eat an entire box of frosting covered cakes. That was twelve cakes. I am not sure how I kept from getting sick, but I didn't. Then as I would finish the last cake, I would feel guilty that I had just eaten the entire box. What was I doing? Why did I eat all of them? I didn't know but I also knew that I couldn't stop eating.

I lost my weight using the Weight Watchers program. I think one of the reasons is a successful tool for many women is the weekly accountability. You have to weigh in with someone standing over you writing down your weight. It isn't the honor system that you can fudge a little here and there.

It wasn't until I met Dr. Gray and began to understand our bodies' chemical structure that I understood why I gained weight. When a woman is stressed her level of oxytocin is lowered, this lowers her serotonin and raises her cortisol. Cortisol is the chemical that causes belly fat so when you are out of balance, you are naturally gaining weight around your belly. Seratonin is the chemical that regulates your feeling of calmness. When this is lowered, you feel more anxious and are uptight.

Let me explain oxytocin. Women are in a testosterone filled world now. We are in the work place with primarily men surrounding us and we are asked to perform at higher levels than most men are requested to perform. With all of the testosterone filling our world it is no wonder that our oxytocin levels are lowered.

Oxytocin can be raised by touch and when women talk. Ever wonder why as women we love to talk? We are trying to raise our oxytocin levels which will then raise our searatonin levels and lower our cortisol. So in my best estimation, the more we talk the more weight we lose.

It is more than a trend the number of girlfriend getaways that women are taking these days. It makes good chemical sense. When women get together we are able to talk and when we are on a getaway, we typically get a massage, pedicure other pampering services. Between all the talking we do and the pampering, our oxytocin levels are raised to a much higher level by the time we arrive at home.

As Dr. Gray says, "The partner doesn't have to do much to ring your bell if your oxytocin tank is 85% full when you arrive home." This makes sense and can be traced back to the cave days. During these times women would gather in the camps to visit while they did their daily work and watched the children. They would talk all day long so when the men came home from the hunt the women were relaxed because they had increased their level of oxytocin, raised their level of serotonin and lowered their level of cortisol.

So how does this really work in today's society. I am walking proof of this. I lead a balanced life and I have to work hard to gain weight now. I don't crave sweets. In fact, I can hardly eat sugar now. I don't eat starch and you would think that would be hard for a farm girl that used to win mashed potato eating contests as a child.

My point is that when you are balanced in your life, your body's chemicals are balanced as well. When you know what it takes to raise your oxytocin levels you concentrate on getting your fair dosage each day. Whether this is talking to your girlfriends or talking to other women, it is all part of a routine. If you have a particularly difficult situation, don't call your husband. He will just want to fix things and you know he can't. Also, you just want someone to listen.

So find six girlfriends that you can put on your cell phone speed dial and when you have one of those moments and you are tempted to call your husband, STOP and call one of your girlfriends. You know that she will just listen which is what you want. By the time you get off the phone your oxytocin levels will be raised which will raise your serotonin levels and you will have lowered your cortisol. So by the time you arrive home you will look and feel more balanced and you will not have the food cravings that you normally do when you are out of chemical balance. Your husband will likely comment on how well you look and he will think that he had something to do with this, which is fine. The bottom line is that you are less stressed and more in control of your own body's chemicals which controls how you feel, your weight and ultimately your energy level.

When I say that I have to work hard to gain weight it is not to impress you but rather to impress upon you the importance of maintaining balance. There was a time when I was out of balance, over weight and out of energy. Hard to believe when you look at me today and I am like the energizer bunny, I just keep going and going and going.

Take time to evaluate your daily life and determine where you can start adding in girlfriend talking time. When can you start to regain control of your body's chemicals? This is one of the key drivers in your ultimate success in this world. You must have a strong physical body in order to achieve all you can be.

Success Tip: Balance is not easily achieved and it typically takes us being out of balance before we know what we are missing. Isn't it true that we are creatures of pain toleration? We tolerate the level of pain until it reaches a point where we can no longer take it. That threshold is different for each of us. I encourage you to avoid that threshold and become balanced earlier on so that you don't have to suffer as greatly as many other women have suffered.

16

DELEGATE

"Begin doing what you want to do now. We are not living in eternity. We have this moment, sparkling like a star in our hand and melting like a snowflake."

— *Marie Beynon Ray, Author*

ginger rogers

Ginger had a strong work ethic. That combined with the fact that she was a woman and in general, women often have a difficult time delegating. Women tend to believe they are super heroes and can conquer the world in one swoop twice as fast as men. So, why would they delegate?

That is a challenge that women faced in Ginger's time and still face today. Not much has changed. For Ginger, she just kept plugging away. In general, costume fittings were usually done after the day's shooting, which meant that Ginger didn't usually get home before nine. It was tough working those long hours. She decided to ask the studio to make an exception and allow her to have her fittings done on the set during the shooting. Ginger thought this was a great solution, but even that was too hectic because she had to rush off the stage into the portable dressing room. Then a wardrobe lady would whip Ginger out of her filming costume into another one that had to be fitted. Because she had to stand and be tugged and pinned all the while, this broke her train of thought for the character. Then she would have to change back into her filming dress to return to the set where the director always seemed to be tapping his pencil waiting for her. And, that was her resting time so there was no rest.

After three months of this hectic rushing, Ginger decided she had enough. She went to the studio and asked to delegate her fittings. She asked them to put in a double for her that would stand in for the fittings while Ginger would watch. That way Ginger could provide comments and feedback without losing her train of thought. She could also sit and rest a bit since that was the only break she was getting.

The studio reluctantly accepted her idea and she was able to make her schedule more manageable. As a woman, we tend to do just what Ginger did. We keep accepting it for what it is. We believe we are tough enough to stick it out and also believe that someone else will not be open to the option of delegation. Just as Ginger proved, all you have to do is ask and take the initiative. It is the first step that is always the hardest yet can be the most gratifying. I can't imagine how gratifying it was for Ginger.[xxxi]

dr. john gray

If you have ever read my friend Dr. John Gray's book series, Men are from Mars, Women are from Venus then you will understand the news flash that says, "Men and women are wired differently." I know it is a shock to you, but it is true.

The quicker we learn the differences and how to manage them, the faster we will alleviate stress in our lives. Men's brains are wired differently in that there are two distinct sides. They process things and identify the three things that need to be done, look for their "atta boys" when finished and then go to their cave to rejuvenate. The cave typically involves a 54" or larger television with a remote control.

Then they come out of the cave rejuvenated and ready to tackle the next three tasks and they just need to know when they need to be done.

Women on the other hand don't have a separation line in the brain. Things fire off from both sides and we go back and forth all of the time. That's why we have never ending to-do lists and never seem to be caught up on anything in life. We get up in the morning and are making lists. When we get into the shower we are writing with the shower chalk all of the things we need to get done. By the time we finish our shower, the walls are full and we are stressed as we dry off. We haven't even started the day but the list has gotten longer.

When your husband asks what you are doing that day, you go off. You rant and rave rattling off all of the things on your never ending to-do list. You think that he is not listening because he pipes in to ask a question about number four on your list and you are already on number twenty four. You accuse him of not listening when in reality, he is just trying to figure out the three things you want him to do and by when. And all you are doing is venting about your never-ending to-do list.

This situation has caused just as many and maybe more arguments in households across this country than sex or money, which are the two top reasons men and women argue. What are you to do? How do you manage this? I recommend delegating.

Take a blank sheet of paper and draw a line down the middle. In the right hand column write down everything that you do every week that only you can do. Then in the left hand column write down everything that you do that could be delegated. When you have finished I have a challenge for you. Because we all think we are a prima donna princess, you no doubtedly have a longer list on the left than you should. Go back through every listing that you believe you and only you can do. Ask yourself if that is really the case or if you just think that. Move more tasks over to the right hand column.

Now you are ready to start delegating. Pull the top three things you want your spouse to do and then tell him when you want them done. I'm not sure how your house runs but it typically takes my husband three times as long to do a task as it does me. For example I can go to the market, pick up dry cleaning, stop by the bank and pick out a birthday present in 27 minutes. O.K. It might be 29 minutes if a hit the stop light.

My husband will take three hours to do these same tasks and will call me five times. I used to get aggravated and think , oh my gosh, what's the use. I can do it myself and save time and that hassle of the phone calls. But the motto I adopted years ago still holds true.

Just because I can doesn't mean I should.

Who cares if it takes him five hours to do these tasks. The point is that they are off of my list and it saved me time and energy. I was freed up to work on something else. Just as importantly, my husband feels that he is contributing and doing something to make my life easier. And, let's face it, that is what they want to do in life. Make our lives easier and make us happy. I know it sounds corny, but it is true.

What I do now is adopt a specific task list. Each day I think of the things that I need to have done that I don't have time to do myself. I ask my husband to do them. He usually grumbles about it but when he is finished I give him the "atta boys" that he deserves. I tell him how much time it saved me and what it meant to me to have him do it. Then he goes to his cave to rejuvenate and is ready for the next three things on the list.

When I read through Dr. Gray's book, I thought it was somewhat silly. Then I started listening to him and his team and I realized that he may have a point. Once I started using the basic principles it was amazing how much my relationship improved. My husband and I will celebrate our seventeenth wedding anniversary in 2009. He is my best friend, my confidant, my love and my soul mate.

I think of how much richer our lives are because I learned how men and women are wired differently. This is not only applicable in your personal life but also in your professional life. Men are wired the same at home and in business.

The quicker you learn to delegate and present information in a fashion that men can understand, the more successful you will be. If you start running down a complete list of all the things you are going to accomplish, you will lose the men in the room. They want to know the three things they need to get done and by when. Once they have those completed they are onto the next three.

Success Tip: Remember that we all process information differently and your new motto should be: Just because I can, doesn't mean I should.

17

ARE YOU MENTALLY FIT & DO YOU HAVE THE SUPPORT TEAM AROUND YOU?

"The impossible: what nobody can do until somebody does."
— *Anonymous*

ginger rogers

There are situations that each of us are thrust into that test our abilities and our mental adeptness. Focus is a key asset that is possessed by few people yet is tried and tested when you least expect it.

Ginger was invited to the White House by President Franklin D. Roosevelt as the one motion picture star to honor the president. The phone call came to her mother and she delivered the invitation to Ginger. When her mother arrived at the house and shared the invitation, Ginger replied saying, "Don't you think he would have asked a Democrat and not a Republican?" Then she paused. She wasn't sure that she wanted to accept the invitation. Not because she wasn't Democrat, but because she was about to start on a six week vacation and she really didn't like to travel, D.C. was a long trip, especially in those days.

Then she realized the tremendous honor that had been bestowed upon her with this request. She couldn't say no. So, she rearranged her entire schedule and had her mother accompany her to Washington, D.C. They arrived and were hustled to the Mayflower Hotel where they only had about an hour to get ready for the evening's festivities. This was a short amount of time after having ridden the train all that distance.

They hurried around and prepared for the evening. They were whisked off to the White House where they were seated next to the Secretary of Labor in the Oval Office. People were bustling all around the office. Radio men were clamoring around the President and announced that they would be on air in approximately twelve minutes. The President looked right at Ginger and then called one of his aids to his side. He whispered something and then the aid approached Ginger. He simply said, "The President would like you to dance for him."

Ginger was shocked and then immediately went to the reality of the situation. The Oval Office had a two inch thick plush rug on the floor. "Where am I supposed to dance?" The aid simply pointed to a small piece of marble flooring. "There," he said. Ginger had a stunned expression on her face as she got up to walk toward the minuscule piece of marble floor.

It was difficult just to walk on the plush rug with her long gown, slits up the side and high heels. But she made her way to the small piece of flooring and then she realized how slippery it was. Nervousness had already overcome her now reality set in and she was immediately aware that she could easily slip and fall on this small piece of flooring.

Her form fitted gown was gorgeous and had two shoulder straps. One showcased the beautiful orchid corsage that had been given to her by the President's birthday committee. She heard the music and started to move in a graceful manner. Then, the announcer broke in saying, "And now we come to you from San Francisco." The waltz was immediately replaced by a break neck speed song. The rhythm was truly wild and Ginger couldn't possibly keep up. Striving to come to a middle ground with the rhythm, she danced dangerously close to the thick rug and in whirling she lost her balance. She didn't fall, but the strap on her gown slipped off her shoulder and as she quickly grasped her dress, but she wasn't fast enough. The crowd of people in the Oval Office had gotten more than an eye full.

Ginger was embarrassed beyond words yet the audience and the President clapped and cheered. The music had stopped and the President began his radio address. When he was finished, he called Ginger to his desk. He told her that he knew how difficult it must have been for her to be put on the spot like that and to overcome the challenges of the floor and circumstances. He expressed his sincere gratitude for her accommodating his request and then handed her his radio address, which he had signed. Ginger later learned that she had one of the very few copies of a radio address that President Roosevelt had allowed to leave the Oval Office.

Ginger was truly put on the spot. However, she had practiced for so many years that unbeknownst to her, she was mentally and physically prepared to handle a situation such as this. She may have looked nervous to her mother, but deep inside she was mustering the mental capacity to dance her best for the President.

You never know when you will be given a chance so you have to train yourself mentally and physically to be ready at all times. It takes fortitude, dedication and commitment to achieve the ultimate in greatness. You will not know you are there until you are tested just as Ginger was in the ultimate situation.[xxxii]

jackie joyner-kersee

Jacqueline Joyner was born in 1962 and was named Jacqueline after
President Kennedy's wife. Jackie Joyner's grandmother said that name was
appropriate because when she took her first look at the tiny baby, she knew
this girl would be the first lady of something.

Jackie's journey was extremely difficult as she braved the tough and mean
streets of East St. Louis every day growing up. She remembers sitting in the
corner of their wallpaper and stick home telling her sister that they were going
to make it. Make it out and make things different.

That was certainly easier said than done. When Jackie was eleven, she saw a
man gunned down right outside the front door of their home. Then just a few
days later, she spoke to her grandmother on the telephone only to find out the
next day that her grandfather had gotten drunk and shot her while she was
sleeping.

Jackie's mother, Mary, made a strict rule that Jackie could not date until she
was eighteen. Mary did not want her to fall into the same trap that her and Al
Joyner had. They were married when Mary was sixteen and Al was fifteen.
She knew Jackie was growing up fast, but didn't want her to grow up that
fast. It took mental fitness and strength but Jackie managed to avoid drugs,
alcohol and boys.

Jackie focused her time and energy on sports and school. She was a gifted
athlete even at an early age. She graduated high school in the top ten percent
of her class and then went west to UCLA. She played basketball there and
also began competing in track and field.

Freshman year in college is tough enough, but for Jackie it got even tougher. She received a phone call just half way through her freshman year. It was her father and he explained that Mary, her mother, had been struck with a rare form of meningitis.

Jackie immediately went to her mother's bed side, but it was too late. She was stricken with this tragedy only to be told that she needed to be the one to take her mother off life support because her father couldn't bear to do it. Jackie was grief stricken as she took her mother off life support and watched her mother die at the young age of thirty seven.

When Jackie returned to UCLA, she was offered comfort by her track coach, Bob Kersee, who explained that he had also lost his mother at a young age. He is the one that saw her true athletic potential in track and field and became her trainer. With Jackie he was like a drill sergeant on the field and then a tender loving man off the field. With his comfort, she was able to rely on her own mental fitness to get her through these tough times. She had been building and strengthening her mental fitness since she was a child.[xxxiii]

It was his training of her coupled with her mental fitness that set her on the historical Olympic Gold Medal winning streak. Jackie is the heptathlon world record-holder and American record-holder in the long jump, this despite her diagnosis with asthma. She spent many years in denial and didn't want to tell her coaches. She had full blown attacks and would have to wear masks when she was competing. She was afraid that her coaches would think she was just out of shape. Mentally she overcame the fear and started taking the appropriate medications to help her. As her grandmother predicted at Jackie's birth, she became the first lady of something: track and field.

Then the criticism came. Critics accused her of using drugs to enhance her athletic performance. Jackie never failed a drug test and still holds strong that she did not use performance enhancing drugs. [xxxiv]

Jackie retired in 1998 but she doesn't look back. She believes, "It is better to look ahead and prepare than to look back and regret."

Most believe that to be an Olympic athlete the person needs to be fit. The emphasis is placed on being physically fit and there is less emphasis placed on being mentally fit. Yet it is the mental game that is a significant factor in determining an athletes' success.

Jackie Joyner-Kersee is an example of how important mental fitness is. If she hadn't started developing this at an early age, she would not be the historic icon that she. [xxxv]

my story

The phrase from my friend Les Brown is appropriate here. If you are the smartest one in your circle of friends, then you need a new circle of friends. We are only challenged when we expand our views, our relationships and expose ourselves to a world that we are not familiar with. Then and only then can we actually see and experience what is possible.

We have to be pushed to do so. Only 10% of people that purchase a book will read past chapter two so the fact that you are on this chapter tells me that you are an over-achiever. Now that we have established this fact, what do you do to push yourself? I struggle with this every day. I have extremely high expectations of myself and of others. So much so that the expectations are usually unrealistic. Yet, I find that performing at 60% is still more than most people's 100%. That's what us overachievers do, that is how we are wired.

When you are in this situation, how do you keep yourself motivated and challenged to go to the next level? What is it that pushes you and drives you to do and be more? You cannot solely rely on yourself because if you do, you will continually accept 60% and never perform at 100% let alone 150%. That means that you are constantly depriving the world of the additional 40% to 110% of what you are here on this earth to contribute.

I certainly am not an advocate of becoming a work-aholic. Yet there are ways to manage things properly and still perform at your potential. Who do you turn to? Who do you call upon? I recommend that you find a HeadGames Specialist. Yes this is a true profession. You see, your brain and performance abilities can be viewed as muscles. They need to be built and trained for the ultimate in performance. In this situation, you would view your head games specialist as a personal mental trainer. Helping you build the mental muscles that you need to perform at your potential and achieve all that you want to achieve.

We so often hire the personal trainer to help us physically perform at an optimum level or look our best, but we do not treat our mental muscles with the same discipline and respect. Many may work with a life coach, but there is a difference between a professional head games trainer. It is Olympic athlete training for your mental game. I first experienced this several years ago and learned that optimum performance is driven by strong discipline. You have to build your mental muscles and tighten them just as you do your physical muscles. This is only achieved through high-performance mental trainers.

When you get yourself into a training routine and are disciplined to continue to stretch even more, you will see ultimate results and be performing at an optimum level. Remember, this is a training program. Olympic athletes do not achieve their status overnight. Championship teams do not achieve that level of accomplishment without constant training, tremendous discipline and the right support system.

My question to you is simple. Do you want to be average or do you want to achieve ultimate greatness for yourself? The kind of greatness that creates a warming sensation in the pit of your stomach because you know you have arrived, you have achieved and you are in your element. Remember, that is achieved when you reach optimum performance levels which takes training. Are you ready to be trained? Are you willing to stretch? Are you ready to experience pain and burst through the pain thresholds that it will take to achieve greatness?

Success Tip: You have to be mentally prepared because this is the game of your life. How you train for it and the attitude you bring when the game of life is on will determine your legacy. This is the ultimate impact you leave on this world.

18

Never Judge a Book by its Cover – There may be a Treasure Inside

"Invest in a human soul. Who knows? It might be a diamond in the rough."
— *Mary McLeod Bethune, educator*

ginger rogers

Ginger Rogers was a Hollywood movie star and a legend on Broadway. She recounted a vivid memory of traveling with her mother to see her grandfather. They arrived by train and as Ginger got off the train, her grandfather gave her a disgusted and angry look. She couldn't figure it out since she thought he would be ecstatic to see her.

Ginger's mother was pulled aside and given the third degree. It turns out her grandfather was devastated and angry that Ginger got off the train looking like an ordinary girl. He had been touting to all the neighbors and town folk that Ginger, his granddaughter, was a movie star and would be coming to visit. He expected her to get off the train in a long flowing chiffon gown with a large picture perfect hat. He didn't understand that Ginger preferred to keep things simple when she could.

She tried to explain to her grandfather that she may have become famous but she was still his granddaughter, the same little girl who had lived with him and walked hand in hand with him to the grocery store and delighted in the penny candies he would buy her. It was still Virginia standing in front of him, she had just grown up.

He didn't understand. He was judging the book by its cover and she didn't look like a movie star to him and certainly wouldn't to his friends and neighbors. Her grandfather said in a disheartened voice, "But, Grand-baby, how do you think I feel? All of the neighbors know your coming to visit me and they're expecting a movie star, not an ordinary girl. You're supposed to be like an orchid. You're supposed to be different. Who wants to see an ordinary field flower or buttercup or daisy? Everybody expects you to look like a movie star. You are a star!"

Ginger couldn't believe that her grandfather was so angry with her based upon her appearance. She still felt the same inside but her grandfather didn't want Virginia Katherine McMath, he wanted Miss Ginger Rogers. That was a hard moment for Ginger as she realized that even if she kept her feet on the ground, others would try to put her on a pedestal for their own purposes. She told her grandfather that she could only be what she was and that wouldn't change no matter what clothing she was wearing.

How often do we judge a book by its cover? Even family can do that even though we all know that it's what is inside that truly matters. Yet that doesn't always hold true, even with family.[xxxvi]

cathie black

Cathie Black had made a name for herself in the print media world. She leveraged her connections and her extensive relationships over the years and they paid off when she was offered the position of President then at the new publication, USA Today.

Faced with a challenge of weak sales for advertising space, Cathie set up a meeting with a longtime ad man in New York. He had recently left a large creative shop and formed his own. Her goal for the meeting was to convince him that the USA Today was the place for him to direct some of the advertising buys of his clients.

The conversation took quite a different turn when Cathie asked him what he thought of the USA Today's own advertising campaigns. He quickly replied saying, "They suck. Your publication is fantastic, but you'd never know it from looking at those ads! I should be doing your campaign."

Cathie acknowledged that their advertising wasn't where it needed to be yet she wondered how she could pull the campaign from an internationally acclaimed advertising agency and give it to a small, no name shop. Over the next day or so, Cathie realized that one thing was apparent. This man was fired up about her publication, he believed in the publication and he was excited about the campaign. That was in fact more than she could say about the existing firm.

She knew that the snobby Ivy League executives from the global advertising agency probably commuted into the meetings hiding her publication in their briefcase out of sheer embarrassment. That's how little clout that paper had in the early days.

She knew this was true, but how could she recommend dumping such an iconic firm and recommend this tiny little shop? She thought it would be crazy to invite this small shop to come in and do a presentation, then she thought it would be crazy not to. The advertising creative was the most important element at the end of the day. That was the end goal, but what if this small shop could not deliver?

She decided to go rogue and called the small agency. She requested that George come up with some ideas and present them to her in her office. He did and what he presented was fresh and free of in-your-face humor. She knew that she had found the agency that could create the campaign they needed.

Then there was the tricky part. She had put out the search to George's small agency on her own. She knew that she wanted to suggest this fresh, new idea yet still had a fear that people would think it was a dumb idea. She quickly overcame this when she realized that she knew, with complete confidence that this was the firm, the campaign and it would work for the newspaper.

As she presented the concept of opening up to an outside small firm, her boss was surprised. This came out of the blue just one day before the global iconic agency was going to present. She explained all about George and his small advertising agency. He quickly reassured her that they had brought her in for new ideas and so she should do just that. Bring in the new ideas.

The next day it was apparent that the large agency was not excited. The ads that were presented did not capture the energy of this bold paper. As the agency's team left the room, Cathie asked her team to stay seated. She explained that she had requested George Lois make a presentation. Everyone in the room asked who he was. No one had heard of him. Cathie thought to herself, "You are about to find out."

George entered the room and gave an Academy Award winning performance. When he was finished with the entire presentation the room was completely silent. Everyone sat speechless as Cathie's heart pounded. What if they didn't like the campaign? She knew the ads were good, but what if they didn't think so. Finally one man on her team piped up and said, "Welllll, George, I don't know much about New York ad agencies, but those ads are the first ones I've seen that seem exactly right for USA Today." Then all heads shifted and eyes were focused on Cathie's boss. He simply said, "We've got it."[xxxvii]

What if Cathie had judged the book by its cover? George's advertising agency was certainly small and at that time he was a "no name." If she had blown off his enthusiastic request to work on the campaign, Cathie and the paper would have missed out on a tremendous advertising campaign. It breathed the life back into what they were doing for their own advertising. Never judge a book by its cover because you may very well find a hidden treasure inside. That's certainly what happened to Cathie.

my story

I remember vividly having received an introduction to a man through a friend of mine. I was on deadline and it took me two weeks to contact him. I didn't worry about it since I was approaching him to solicit his advertising agency to do my work. When I called him, he was rude and read me the riot act for taking two weeks to get back to him.

I was professional and polite as we set a time to meet for coffee. Yet I remember when I hung up the phone, I could not believe the conversation I had just had. I was doing him a favor by meeting with him and allowing him to bid on my project yet he made me justify why I hadn't been able to get back to him.

I was determined that I would give the guy 15-minutes maximum as a courtesy to my friend that referred me. After that, I had no time for someone that would speak to me in that tone of voice when he wanted my business. I was the potential customer.

I remember meeting one morning and as I approached the table and he was sitting there with another young man. They stood up and shook my hand. As we started the conversation, they quickly realized that I had a strong advertising background and clearly understood how agencies worked as well as what went into a successful branding campaign.

The more Eric—the younger man—spoke, the more I felt a connection. He understood what I wanted to accomplish and he had a strong portfolio. His small firm had done work with Fortune 500 companies globally. It was quality work and he saw my vision.

After nearly two hours in that meeting, I left thinking that I was certainly glad that I didn't judge this book by the cover and the impression that Dave left on me. If I had, I would have sold myself short and would have deprived my business of the advertising agency services that were creatively provided by a boutique firm with heart.

We are certainly in a society that is driven by first impressions. It is often difficult not to judge someone by their appearance or the first words out of their mouth. Yet so many people have been proven wrong when they look under the hood and see what type of company or person is really behind the façade.

Success Tip: Following the feeling you have when you first meet a new client or potential business deal is one way to find that hidden treasure. Don't be mislead by the appearance of the size of a company. Bigger is not always better and smaller doesn't always mean antiquated.

19

Never Give Up

" I want to be good, and when it is all over not to have the feeling that I might have done better."
— *Ruth St. Dennis*

ginger rogers

Ginger was tough. She kept plugging along no matter what her schedule and what the situation. During one film, the scene had been set where Ginger was upset with Fred. She ran into the bathroom to wash her hair and Fred approached the piano and began to sing The Way you Look Tonight. Ginger was to come out of the bathroom with her hair full of bubbly shampoo.

Yet the shampoo was a problem. She tried it and every time she would near the piano, the soap would be running into her eyes and the bubbles would have disappeared. She looked terrible and felt even worse. They tried all types of soap and nothing worked. They even tried shaving cream. To no avail, Ginger was soaked in soapy scum and frustrated.

Someone suggested whipped cream and so they had a stage hand run to the commissary to grab some whipped cream. They piled it on her head and it worked. She had a frothy cap that appeared to be shampoo and they made it through the scene. The minute they were finished with that take, she had to run to her dressing room, wash her hair and re-do her make-up in order to do the last scene.

The last dance number in this film, "Never Gonna Dance," was a difficult one because Fred was on one side of the screen and Ginger was on the other side. The scene was set in a night club and they had to dance together and then each of them whirled up eighteen steps to the second floor where they danced and danced and danced. They did over forty-eight takes and danced into the wee hours of the morning. Everything that could have gone wrong did from noise in the camera to a missed step in the dance to even one take where Fred's toupee flipped off.

During this entire debacle, Ginger never said a word about her own problem. Her feet were really hurting her. During one of the breaks she went to the sidelines and took off her shoes. They were filled with blood. She had danced her feet raw. One of the men saw this and was shocked and appalled that her feet were so bloody. He offered to stop the shooting. Ginger refused. She was not going to give up and be the cause of delaying the filming. They finally got a good take and called it a wrap at 4 am. Ginger was then able to take her bloody feet home.

It would have been much easier for Ginger to give up especially with the physical pain that she was enduring. Yet, she was not about to give up. She mustered up the courage and mental ability to block the pain in order to keep going. And it worked. This film was a success in every way possible. What if she would have postponed the last take? Would they have been able to recreate the chemistry that they had going at that point? Would the dance routine have had the same appeal? She insisted on plowing through at all costs and she was glad that she did. That is how Ginger handled her entire career. She always found the courage to keep going and never gave in, no matter what pain and suffering she was experiencing.[xxxviii]

lucille ball

In 1938 at the age of twenty-seven, Lucille Ball was miserable and more isolated from people than ever before. She was getting worthless parts and it felt to her as if these parts were being dredged up from the bottoms. She told people that she was happy being the "queen of B's"(B- rated films) but she really wasn't happy with her roles and she pined for more even if it meant breaking away from RKO studios where she had been.

She reached the point of sheer exhaustion and collapsed while filming Dance, Girl, Dance after she had spent tireless hours each day filming and then countless hours at night rehearsing the dance scenes. She was living on junk food, cocktails and smoking like a freight train. She recovered and managed to give an electrifying performance in the movie's last scene.

It was during that time she ran into Desi Arnaz at the commissary. She overheard him stating clearly that he did not like Lucy's acting and did not want to be cast opposite her as the studio was pitching. She went about her business and a few days later Desi saw her again and she certainly took his breath away as she was wearing a flattering yellow sweater and beige slacks. He went up to her and introduced himself. Lucy was not impressed and bantered with him joking about his name. She twisted it in all directions from calling him Dizzy to Daisy.

It was truly love at first site and they ended up doing the movie Too Many Girls together. Desi began calling her Lucy and they started spending countless hours together. The movie and Lucy's performance received glowing reviews yet Desi's performance did not. Even though she received rave reviews, her agent was struggling with the studios to get approval on her contract for a measly $500 per week. They considered her poison to the box office.

They were going off of the Gallup poles which showed that 40 percent of all theater goers said they had never seen Lucy even though she had appeared in over thirty five movies. Only 33 percent of the people could identify Lucy from a photograph. Audience comments ranged from calling her cheap to common to vulgar and coarse.

She was distraught and frustrated wondering if anyone would ever discover her true talent and embrace her for who she really was. She and Desi had been married for a while at this point and owned a property but the commute and distance was growing between their two careers. It certainly didn't help that she was tired of being a B-rated actress. She was bored and extremely frustrated.

She never gave up but those were certainly volatile times between her and Desi. She kept plugging away and somehow stayed focused on what she wanted. She knew that some day there would be something for her. She didn't know what, but she just had to stick it out long enough. They fell on hard times, had financial difficulties in addition to hectic schedules.

Through it all, she never gave up. After having suffered through the hectic schedules and numerous two bit movie parts, Lucy was committed to doing something on television. The schedules would be better suited for her and Desi and she had the wild idea of adapting their comedic radio skit for television. All the major networks hated the idea. They could not conceive of a Latin man on television with a Caucasian woman. Lucy was relentless and determined not to give up.

Lucy was reported to have had Carole Lombard (who had been killed in a plane crash) come to her in a dream and tell her, "Honey, go ahead. Take a chance. Give it a whirl." And Lucy did. She and Desi formed Desilu Company and they fought tooth and nail to create a program that featured the two of them, provided a comedic relief and was shot in front of a live audience. All things that were not normal at that time.

In order to make it work, they had to film a pilot program. They didn't have the money themselves, but Lucy was committed so she got creative and they borrowed $5,000 from the General Amusement Corporation. That was the agency that Lucy and Desi had toured with in vaudeville. Lucy and Desi scraped every penny they had and matched the funds. They hired the writers that had helped them with the "My Favorite Husband" program. They completed the pilot and CBS told them the only way they would be interested was if there were a sponsor. No sponsor, no deal.

The pilot was pitched to at least six agencies and all turned the sponsorship opportunity down. Finally the pilot was brought to an agency whose primary client was Philip Morris cigarettes and it turned out they were looking for new sponsorship opportunities. They struggled with the name because it was suggested that they call the show the Lucille Ball Show. She was furious that Desi's name was not in the title so they appeased her and told her to call the show the Lucille Ball and Desi Arnez Show. Still upset at the thought that Desi was receiving second billing someone finally came up with the idea of the I Love Lucy show. She was pleased with that because she believed that once people watched the show they would realize that the "I" stood for Desi Arnez so he would receive top billing which was important to Lucy.

They agreed and the studio was pleased there was a sponsor. But that was just the beginning of the challenges. Desi had a wild idea to film the scenes on a movie set in a studio which at that time did not accommodate the number of people they wanted in the audience. They bucked the system and found a studio, were ready to shoot the first scene when the authorities came in and shut them down because they did not have a separate women's and men's bathroom. They had to scramble and convert Lucy's dressing room bathroom into the women's public restroom. The taping continued and ended up over budget by $250,000 and the studio was chomping at the bit.

They did test runs and received rave laughter from the audience but the real test was the first airing on television. It received warm reviews yet the president of the Phillip Morris Company was not amused. He requested that the agency get them out of the Lucy contract. Somehow the agency executives convinced him to hold on until after the second show was aired. They were right and the program took off. It rose quickly in popularity and the race was on.

They had a grueling schedule, even though this was supposed to involve less time. Lucy became a maniac perfectionist. After having been denied her due recognition for all those years in the movies, she now was experiencing the recognition and fame she felt she deserved. So she became a fanatic about all details and making every episode perfect. She drove people crazy on the set including Desi.

She was determined to give it her all and overcame injuries suffered in rehearsal and tireless hours in the studio to continue to make each episode the best she could. It was in 1952 when Lucy finally received the recognition she deserved and fell into the career she was destined to have. That was thirteen years that she had spent trying, trying and trying. She never gave up and it would have been much easier many of those days for her to have given up. Especially during those times when women's roles were clearly different than they are today. How many years have you spent trying to get what you want? She spent what seemed a lifetime for her and didn't really start her career until she was 40 years young. How young are you? Are you ready to give up? You can't. That is not an option no matter what your age.[xxxix]

my story

Since my Crap Out Date when I realized my true passion, I have been relentlessly working towards my goals. It hasn't been easy, but nothing in life that is worth it comes easy. I recall presenting the Power-Injected Marketing toolkit to an internationally recognized author and public speaker. He reviewed the product and liked it. That sparked a conversation about a speaking tour and affiliate agreement. As the conversation concluded and I got on the elevator, I was dumbfounded wondering where I would get the capital to pay for the inventory that I would need on hand in order to make the deal work.

I had put every last dime I had into getting the product tested and now we were ready to go to market with an opportunity of a lifetime. I had no equity left in my home, a car that I was paying for and no credit lines. It felt like I was playing Texas Holdem' and I was all in betting on the cards I had in my hand. I knew they were good, but had no way to ante up to win the pot. At that particular moment, I remember feeling distraught and discouraged. I felt like I had no way to capitalize on an opportunity that came out of the blue and was derived from sheer will and guts. I had played big to make the meeting happen and it worked. How was I going to deliver? How embarrassing to have to go back to these people and admit that I could not fulfill what I had presented.

It would have been easier for me to give up knowing that I had tried, but I couldn't do that. I racked my brain, visited with my banker and finally called a man that I worked with when I first started my career in the hotel industry. We had kept in touch loosely speaking once or twice per year, but I knew that he was experienced in putting real estate deals together.

I thought that if nothing else, he could help me figure out options for capitalization. After all I knew that the traditional bank loan was not going to work because I didn't have a physical inventory that was of value to collateralize the loan.

As we sat and visited over lunch, I explained what I was working on and the opportunities that I was faced with. I explained my challenges and as we were talking, ideas kept coming out. Finally he said, work up a business plan and let me look at the deal. Turns out he had just sold off a hotel development deal and had cash that he was looking to invest. He knew me and how driven I was so he was at least willing to review a plan.

Had I given up before that lunch, I would not have solidified an angel investor deal that fueled the launch of my product and the company. When times seem the bleakest are when the best solutions arise. Bleak situations cause us to become extremely resourceful, more humble and turn to others for help and advice. Not knowing what to expect just looking for advice is a great space to be in. That way you are never disappointed.

I had never worked through a funding deal so needless to say, I spent three months learning, creating documents and working diligently to get the deal done. According to many, that was a record time to close an angel investment deal and I am thankful that I never gave up.

As I look back, I think that I am much like Lucy. I am determined to make it work no matter what. I had spent enough years stifled and knew that what I had created was good. I always figure out a way. Come Hell or high water. Now, if I run into a snag, I reflect back on those days and use the situation to motivate me to continue on the course. We are not always given the answers immediately to our problems but with faith and sheer determination an answer will be revealed.

Success Tip: The thrill of completion far outweighs the feeling of defeat. When you think you can't go any further, look for support and push ahead. Each time you feel like giving up, talk to someone you trust and purge the negative thoughts. Stating this allows you to get the negativity out of your head, allowing you to move forward.

GET ON THE FUN BUS OF LIFE

"Take time to laugh – it is the music of the soul. Take time to be friendly – it is the road to happiness."

— *Author unknown*

ginger rogers

Ginger Rogers was known for having fun. In fact, there was one particular movie that seemed to be written just for Ginger. It was called In Person. Katherine Hepburn turned down the leading lady role and Fred Astaire quickly dismissed it as well. Many in Hollywood believed that the person that took the role would look foolish. Had the role been written for a man it would not have had the humor that it did being written for a woman.

Ginger agreed that Katherine Hepburn was right, the part would have been ridiculous for her. She would have looked idiotic with the false teeth that the plot required. Neither Fred nor Katherine had the absurd sense of humor which made it simple for Ginger to look ridiculous and she did look ridiculous in this film.

This was par for Ginger. She always knew how to have fun both on set and off the set. She had a great sense of humor and did not have any problem expressing this bizarre humor. Ginger loved what she did and it appears that she had fun every day. I believe that is a key attitude that attributed to her tremendous success over the years. Having fun every day along with the ability to laugh at yourself are two admirable qualities.[xl]

ellen degeneres

Ellen was born in New Orleans, Louisiana in 1958. She was raised in a modest home and had what appears to have been a normal childhood. She did standup comedy and some other minor roles in film but it wasn't until the early 2000's that she stepped into her own greatness.

As I look at it, things started to happen for Ellen after she hosted the Emmy Awards on television. This was in November after the terrorist attacks of September 11, 2001. Everyone was clear that the tone needed to be somber yet also provide viewers a temporary outlet to forget the tragedy at least for a few hours. During that program, Ellen received numerous standing ovations and one of them was for a poignant line, "We're told to go on living our lives as usual, because to do otherwise is to let the terrorists win, and really, what would upset the Taliban more than a homosexual woman wearing a suit in front of a room full of Jews?"

Then in 2003 she aired The Ellen Degeneres Show which has become a hit for her. She launched this at a time when several celebrities were vying for day-time television with talk show formats. Yet in my opinion, Ellen was all about having fun. She stayed true to herself and even today when you watch her show, you can clearly see that she is on the fun bus of life. If she wasn't, she couldn't pull off those wacky games that she has the audience participate in.[xli]

my story

Ellen and all of the women that I have highlighted in this book have one common thread and that is they live on the fun bus of life. Each of us has made a decision to get off the struggle bus and not only get on the fun bus of life, but drive this bus. Let's face it, the bus we are on is a choice. We are faced with that choice every day of our life. I spent enough years on the struggle bus that I will never get on it again.

I have a one way unlimited access pass for the fun bus of life and choose to get on that bus each day I get out of bed. I know that it is not easy. I am just like everyone of you. There are days when I don't feel my best or don't have energy or am just in a funk. But I work very hard to identify those days and stand in the shower longer than usual doing mental self-talk. I have a discussion with myself as to how the day will look for me. I paint the picture and as the water hits my head, I lean back and close my eyes. I picture the day unfolding the way I want it to and I envision it. I feel it from head to toe. I put myself on the fun bus of life and use all of my senses to experience my day. Then, by the time I am out of the shower and drying off, I am in a different mental space.

Throughout the day I also look at tools like the DISC personality profile to reflect on my personality, my tendencies and the traits that I have. Understanding these helps me stay grounded and focused. I try to identify why I am in a funk or feeling a particular way and then I associate it with the personality tendency that I have. For example, I have no patience so if I am in the middle of dealing with an accounting issue or reading financial statements dissecting information, I will feel anxious and fidgety. If I am feeling angry it could be because my competitive streak is showing up and my driver personality trait is taking over. If that is the case, then I use this feeling of anger to fuel my energy and push me forward to become the "come back kid." I end up more focused and committed than before.

Whatever tricks you need to adopt, do so. Life is too short for us to be on the struggle bus every day. If you aren't having fun then you should go home because no one will want to be around you, do business with you or talk to you. I challenge you to reflect each day on your fun factor of life and raise the bar. Determine on a scale of one to ten where you are today and then write down where you want to be. Then challenge yourself and identify the specific actions that you will need to take to get to that level of fun in your life.

It starts by making a concerted effort each and every day. Even on those days when you really don't feel like it. Those are the most critical days for you to push yourself and do laugh aerobics. One technique that I have adopted is when a situation arises, I pause, laugh and then start to handle it. By laughing I found that I trigger my brain and confuse myself. I am then able to look at the situation without being tainted. I have increased the oxygen flow in my body and I am better prepared to handle it, no matter how bad it is. Choose to laugh even when you really want to cry. It will increase the oxygen flow and help you handle the situation.

Success Tip: Are you on the fun bus of life? What is your fun factor? If you are not where you want to be, the first step is awareness. Be aware of where you are at, know where you want to be and just as you do with anything else you want to achieve, create an action plan to go after it. Fun is not trivial and is a worthwhile goal to achieve. Raise your fun factor in life and cheers to being a more empowered woman. You'll be surprised at the way people around you begin to lighten up when you are the chief fun-leader in a group, meeting, conference or office.

Well Behaved Women Rarely Make History

"Sugar coating is for cereal, so if you want Cocoa Puffs, eat them for breakfast."
— *Sheila Stewart*

ginger rogers

Ginger was dating George Gershwin and would often spend weekends together in Hollywood, Palm Springs or other nearby cities. They enjoyed each other's company and always had fun together. One particular evening Ginger decided to surprise George at the restaurant. She talked with Fred ahead of time and they both agreed to do an impromptu dance routine in public that evening for George.

As the orchestra started to play, Ginger got up and met Fred on the dance floor. They acknowledged George and then began to dance. They floated across the floor as they usually did with the grace, elegance and the style of true professionals. Until Ginger hit a spot of liquid and Fred had to catch her before she hit the floor. George was truly touched that they would dance for him, especially in public. Fred and Ginger had never danced in public so this was a special evening.

That Saturday afternoon Ginger and George drove to Pasadena to see a football game and on the way back to Hollywood, George asked Ginger if he could stop at an art store to pick up some things. Turns out it was some of George's paintings that he had left for framing. She was thrilled to have the opportunity to see some of his work. While he was dealing with the shop keeper, Ginger poked around and browsed through the store. She lifted the lid on a wooden box and stared at a gorgeous set of pastels in a rainbow of colors. She admired them and thought of the fun she could have working with them.

While she was admiring them, George reappeared with his paintings and settled with the shop keeper. She got in the car and George loaded the last painting. As he got in the car he handed her a wrapped box. He had given her the large box of pastel chalk that she was admiring in the store.

When they returned to George's house, he started to paint and Ginger watched diligently over his shoulder as he made every stroke on the canvas. She decided to do some sketching herself and asked if George had a photo of himself that she could sketch with the pastels. He directed her to a table in the next room that had several pictures on it. He told her to pick anyone that she wanted to draw. She found the picture that she liked, but it wasn't of George or Ira. It was Irving Berlin. She sat on the floor in the room next to where George was painting and began to sketch Irving Berlin. She was having fun.

At dinner that night, George told the guests that Ginger certainly had chutzpah. He detailed the story that she had the nerve to sit on the floor of his home and sketch his greatest rival, Irving Berlin. "She must be crazy about me," he said. Ginger did have chutzpah and was not always a well-behaved woman. Both on the set and off the set she certainly was herself. She was independent and didn't always care what others thought of her. I believe that had a positive impact on her career over the years.[xlii]

joan of arc

Joan of Arc came from an obscure village and was an uneducated peasant. She was barely more than a child when her heroics and defiance of society's normalcy made her a legend of her time.

She was born in 1412 in eastern France. She claimed to have first heard voices in her head when she was a young girl about six years old. She claimed that as she grew older, she also had visions from God that told her to recover her homeland from English domination which was late in the Hundred Years' War. Determined and committed to follow the guidance of the vision, she petitioned for permission to travel with the army and wear the equipment of a knight.

This was certainly an exception for that time and it was also defiant for a woman to dress like a man. She cut her hair short and when her petition was granted, she relied upon donated items for her armor, horse, sword, banner and entourage. Many people believed that only a regime that was in the final straits of desperation would pay any heed to an illiterate farm girl who claimed that the voice of God was instructing her to take charge of her country's army and lead it to victory.

It was May of 1430 when Joan of Arc was captured. It happened when she was ordered to retreat and she assumed the honorable place of being last to leave the field. Typically when one was captured, the family would pay the ransom of the prisoner of war. Unfortunately, her family did not have the financial resources for the ransom and King Charles VIII would not come to her aid either.

She certainly didn't give up. She tried to escape but to no avail. Finally the English government purchased her from the Duke of Burgundy. She was then put on trial for heresy which was politically motivated. Pope Callixtus III declared her innocent, but that did not have precedence over the jurisdiction.

Historians have reviewed the trial records and Joan of Arc demonstrated tremendous intellect. She was forced to sign a abjuration document that she did not understand. Her signature was purely under the threat of having to drink unpasteurized milk. Pure torture! They tried hard to diagnose her with numerous mental illnesses to explain the supposed voices she heard in her head.

Joan of Arc remained astute despite the terrible conditions she was confined to and the rigors that she was experiencing. She was convicted and burned at the stake when she was only nineteen years old. Twenty-four years later she was found innocent and she has since been beautified on numerous occasions.
xliii

She certainly was not a well-behaved woman during her time. She stood up for what she believed and went against everything that society in the 1400's said was normal. She defied those around her by dressing like a boy and declaring publicly that the voice and vision of God is what was directing her. Yet we are grateful today that she was not a well-behaved woman. She can be considered one of the pioneering women in the world that proved a woman can speak her mind and does not deserve punishment for merely being different.

my story

This was the most difficult chapter for me to write mainly because I was intimidated by the title. Well Behaved Women Rarely Make History.

Deep down I certainly believe that I am not well-behaved. In fact I probably never have been. Throughout my life I have been encouraged to embrace my unique talents and to honor my opinions. For many, this is not acceptable. Years ago I realized this rebellious streak that I have and I started to embrace it.

What was most difficult for me is the last part of this title – Make History. I don't believe that I have made history and it is hard for me to believe that I have impacted people's lives. Rachel sat across from me as I expressed my discomfort in writing this chapter. I explained how I don't believe I have made history yet and certainly don't believe my efforts compare by any means to those of Joan of Arc and Ginger Rogers. I looked at Rachel and asked her one simple question, "How can I write my section in this chapter when I cannot compare to these historical iconic women?" Rachel's response was interesting to me. It shed new light and gave me another perspective.

She started by correcting me and doing so quickly. She said that I may not be making history in the same way that Joan of Arc did or Ginger Rogers. Yet she explained how I am part of history because I have touched women's lives throughout North America.

I again questioned that and clarified by telling her that I merely speak to women, I don't make history. She again corrected me. (She is a tough one which is why she has been promoted and is a great asset to our company.) What she pointed out was specific instances where she has received phone calls after I have spoken to a group of women. On these phone calls the women explain how their lives have been changed and how much the appreciated the straight-forward approach that I took in explaining key elements that women need in order to be successful.

Then it hit me. I could begin writing this chapter because I may not be making history in the grand fashion as some of the other famous women icons, but I am impacting women entrepreneurs one person at a time. The thought that I could touch, move and inspire women is personally gratifying.

I started reading many of the emails that women have sent me over the last couple of years. These emails were from women that I had only met once. The content ranged from pages and pages of heart pouring, sobbing stories of their crap-out date survival stories to those short and sweet comments stating the profound impact that I had on their lives through my raw honesty.

As I read through these emails, there was one common theme that continued to arise and I hadn't seen it before. I'm not sure why, but it is certainly glaring at me now. These women took comfort thinking that they were not alone. Someone else (meaning me) had spoken and shared personal experiences in business and life, which resonated and struck a chord. The chord was one of camaraderie. Many of these women thought they were the only ones experiencing the difficulty, stress, trauma and physical pains. Yet when they heard my story, they realized that a crap out date is real, it is unfortunately common and it is not fun.

As I reflected on these email messages I cried, I laughed and I had deep admiration for the courage that it took many of these women to write me—a perfect stranger to them. It was sad to me how women are striving to be normal and be accepted when in fact, so many have forgotten that well-behaved women rarely make history.

Before I started this book, I had a strong appreciation for Ginger Rogers yet I didn't realize how similar our lives today are to what she experienced. One would think that after 60 plus years, as women in business and in life, our lives would be much easier and that we would not be dealing with the same issues that Ginger Rogers did. One would think that a not so well-behaved woman such as Ginger would have been able to pave a better path for us.

Yet the path she paved was more like a trail. The type of trail that you often see in grass where a few feet have worn down the grass, but there is no clear and well defined path that is paved with more than a few rebels good intentions.

I recognized that my mission is to give women permission to jump off the band wagon and be abnormal, not normal. It is time we all come together to make history so that we can all pave a path that is solid and clear. One that shows the worn edges to remind women of the sacrifices we made yet gives them enough trail to run, not walk. We don't want others to delay, stumble or fall. We want to give them a clear path that makes it easier for this is how history will be made.

What are you doing? Are you accepting the normalcy that is handed to you by society? Are you accepting that things are the way they are and cannot be improved? I challenge you to go deep inside and find one aspect of your life where you are simply sitting back and playing it safe. Wouldn't you like to make history? Even if it is in your own company or with your own family, you have an opportunity to create a legacy for yourself that of which you and your family can be proud.

You have to stand up to show up to move up.

Are you asleep? Or are you ready to get up? The choice is yours. Just remember that Joan of Arc and Hillary Clinton didn't take their seats calmly and quietly on the bus of life. They stood up to rally those around them to be part of true greatness.

Now I know that I was meant to write this chapter and this book. I am on a mission to help women rally. When we collectively forge ahead as a group of strong entrepreneurs providing each other with the support and encouragement we all need, then we will each help thousands of women make history.

30 Things Every Woman Should Have

by Pamela Redmond Satran

A Woman Should Have......enough money within her control to move out and rent a place of her own, even if she never wants to or needs to

A Woman Should Have......something perfect to wear if the employer, or date of her dreams wants to see her in an hour

A Woman Should Have......a youth she's content to leave behind

A Woman Should Have......a pasty juice enough that she's looking forward to retelling it in her old age

A Woman Should Have......a set of screwdrivers, a cordless drill, and a black bra

A Woman Should Have......one friend who always makes her laugh and one who lets her cry

A Woman Should Have......a good piece of furniture not previously owned by anyone else in her family

A Woman Should Have......eight matching plates, wine glasses with stems, and a recipe for a meal, that will make her guests feel honored

A Woman Should Have......a feeling of control over her destiny

Every Woman Should Know......how to fall in love without loosing herself

Every Woman Should Know......how to quit a job, break up with a lover, and confront a friend without ruining the relationship

Every Woman Should Know......when to try harder and when to walk away

Every Woman Should Know......that she can't change the length of her calves, the width of her hips, or the nature of her parents

Every Woman Should Know......that her childhood may not have been perfect...but it's over

Every Woman Should Know......what she would and wouldn't do for love or more

Every Woman Should Know......how to live alone...even if she doesn't like it

Every Woman Should Know......whom she can trust, whom she can't, and why she shouldn't take it personally

Every Woman Should Know......where to go...be it to her best friend's kitchen table or a charming Inn in the woods when her soul needs soothing

Every Woman Should Know......what she can and can't accomplish in a day, a month, and a year

NOTES

i.   Rogers, Ginger. 1991. Ginger: My Story. New York, NY.
Harper Collins

ii.   Rogers, Ginger. 1991. Ginger: My Story. New York, NY.
Harper Collins

iii.   NBC Today Show- April 2008

iv.   Bucholz, Todd. 2007. New Ideas from Dead CEOs. New York, NY.
Harper Collins

v.   Rogers, Ginger. 1991. Ginger: My Story. New York, NY.
Harper Collins

vi.   Fields, Debra J. 1987. "One Smart Cookie". New York,
NY. Simon & Schuster

vii.   Rogers, Ginger. 1991. Ginger: My Story. New York, NY.
Harper Collins

viii.   Parton, Dolly. 1994. My Life and Unfinished Business. New York,
NY. Harper Collins

ix.   Rogers, Ginger. 1991. Ginger: My Story. New York, NY.
Harper Collins

x.   Axelrod, Alan. 2000. Elizabeth I, CEO: strategic lessons from the
leader who built an empire. New, NY. Prentice Hall Press

xi.   Stewart, Sheila. 2008. 99 Killer Business Ideas from Those Who
Know. Denver, CO. Caboodle Marketing and Publishing

xii.   Rogers, Ginger. 1991. Ginger: My Story. New York, NY.
Harper Collins

xiii.   Lowe, Janet. 1998. Oprah Winfrey Speaks: Insight from the World's Most Influential Voice. New York, NY. John Wiley & Sons Inc.

xiv.   Rogers, Ginger. 1991. Ginger: My Story. New York, NY. Harper Collins

xv.   Walters, Barbara. 2008. Audition: a memoir. New York, NY. Random House

xvi.   Rogers, Ginger. 1991. Ginger: My Story. New York, NY. Harper Collins

xvii.   Bucholz, Todd. 2007. New Ideas from Dead CEOs. New York, NY. Harper Collins

xviii.   Rogers, Ginger. 1991. Ginger: My Story. New York, NY. Harper Collins

xix.   Bernstein, Carl. 2008. A Woman in Charge: The Life of Hillary Rodham Clinton. New York, NY. Random House

xx.   Axelrod, Alan. 2000. Elizabeth I, CEO: Strategic Lessons from the Leader who Built an Empire. New, NY. Prentice Hall Press

xxi.   Rogers, Ginger. 1991. Ginger: My Story. New York, NY. Harper Collins

xxii.   Roberts, Robin. 2007. From the Heart: Seven Rules to Live By. New York, NY. Hyperion

xxiii.   Rogers, Ginger. 1991. Ginger: My Story. New York, NY. Harper Collins

xxiv.   Bucholz, Todd. 2007. New Ideas from Dead CEOs. New York, NY. Harper Collins

xxv. Biography. Sheila Johnson. http://www.answers.com

xxvi. Rogers, Ginger. 1991. Ginger: My Story. New York, NY. Harper Collins

xxvii. Dion, Celine. 2000. My Story My Dream. New York, NY. Harper Collins

xxviii. Rogers, Ginger. 1991. Ginger: My Story. New York, NY. Harper Collins

xxix. Blakely, Sara. 2008. Sara's Story. http://www.spanx.com

xxx. Rogers, Ginger. 1991. Ginger: My Story. New York, NY. Harper Collins

xxxi. Knight, Gladys. 1997. Between Each Line of Pain and Glory: My life Story. New York, NY. Hyperion

xxxii. Rogers, Ginger. 1991. Ginger: My Story. New York, NY. Harper Collins

xxxiii. Rogers, Ginger. 1991. Ginger: My Story. New York, NY. Harper Collins

xxxiv. Schwartz, Larry. Jackie Joyner-Kersee Completes Huge Leap. http://espn.go.com

xxxv. 1995. How Stars Overcame Obstacles. Ebony Magazine

xxxvi. Schwartz, Larry. Jackie Joyner-Kersee completes huge leap. http://espn.go.com

xxxvii. Rogers, Ginger. 1991. Ginger: My Story. New York, NY. Harper Collins xxxviii. Black, Cathie.2007. Basic Black: The Essential Guide for Getting Ahead at Work (and in Life). New York, NY. Random House

xxxix. Rogers, Ginger. 1991. Ginger: My Story. New York, NY. Harper Collins

xl. Higham, Charles. 1986. The Real Life of Lucy Ball. New York, NY. St. Martin's Press

xli. Rogers, Ginger. 1991. Ginger: My Story. New York, NY. Harper Collins

xlii. Wikipedia.2008. Ellen Degeneres. http://en.wikipedia.org/wiki/Ellen_DeGeneres

xliii. Rogers, Ginger. 1991. Ginger: My Story. New York, NY. Harper Collins

xliv. Wikipedia. Joan of Arc. http://en.wikipedia.org/wiki/Joan_of_Arc

xlv. Satara, Pamela Redmond. 1997.Every Woman Should Have. Glamour Magazine, May